Saemaul Undong and Rural Development

Pyeong Ik Choe, Ph.D.
Chi-Sun Oh, Ph. D.
Chan Ho Choi, Ph. D.
Badar N. Siddiqui, Ph. D.

Sanhak Publishing Co. of KICU

Published by : Jong Tae Kim, Ph.D., Samuel Chung, Ph.D.
Edited by : Suk Won Oh
           Sanhak Publishing Co. of KICU

Copyright ©November 10, 2014 by Pyeong Ik Choe, Ph.D.
                         Chi-Sun Oh, Ph.D.
                         Chan Ho Choi, Ph.D.
                         Badar N. Siddiqui, Ph.D.
          576 Chungsin-Ro, Woonkok-Myon, ChungYang-Koon, Choong Nam,
345-872, Seoul, Korea
Printed in the Republic of Korea

Library of Congress Cataloging in Publication Data.
Choe, Pyeong Ik
Oh, Chi-Sun
Choi, Chan Ho
Siddiqui, Badar N.
Saemaul Undong and Rural Development
    1.   Saemaul Undong
    2.   Rural Development
Library of Congress Catalog Card Number

ISBN 978-89-969814-6-6

Preface

This volume provides a set of Korean experience of community development movement; Saemaul Undong.We authors wrote this book as a training manual for the experts working with GOs and NGOs in the field of rural development applied Saemaul Undong in developing countries.

From the above point of view is this manual fills into seven chapters as the follows;
History and community development of Korea, Forerunners of Saemaul Undong. Cooperative heritages such as CCC, Credit Union and Agricultural Cooperatives as well as RDA, et.c. The beginning and evolution of Saemaul Undong. The role ofGOs and NGOs. Strategies, Saemaul education, Achievement and successful factors and Prospectof 21st century, Saemaul Undong's role expectation in the field of ODA.
The importance of practice was emphasized in the last chapter.

In addition,some development strategies and alternatives as countermeasures to challenges of Rwanda were recommended in appendix. Those strategies would be available for the developing countries with similar situation. As Pyeong Ik Choe often said, the lord gives not only challenges but also alternatives. Hence what we have to do is finding the optimal alternatives solving the challenges.

Our wish to see many more volunteers serving to developing countries in Africa, South Asia and Latin America with sweat, tears and prayers were included too.

We tried to pour our studies and experiences in the field of community development as well as Saemaul Undong. However, much remains to be improved.

Our heartily appreciation goesto Dr. Dona of the Philippines for her assistanceand all the cooperation by many friends of various organizations.

November 5, 2014
Authors

Table of Content

I. History and Community Development of Korea

There are similarities and dissimilarities among different cultures. Considering similarities in culture, every society has cooperative activities due to affiliation of human being. For example, the traditional cooperative activities in Indonesia(GotongRoyong :Cooperation which means mutual aid or cooperation among community people to attain a shared goal) are very much similar with those of Korean history and **Umuganda** is Rwandan Saemaul Undong. On the otherhand, we can find many ways of development alternatives chosen by grass-root participants/leaders, and differentials in circumstances including climate, natural resources and neighboring countries. The rise and fall of development in Korean history is also one example of the results from the alternatives decided mainly by the leaders in the history. For a deep understanding of current development of Korea, a brief review of the history, land, cultural identity andtrends of development is suggested.

1. HistoryofKorea

1). Brief History

The Lower Paleolithic era in the Korean Peninsula began roughly half a million years ago. The earliest known Korean pottery dates to around 8000 BC, and the Neolithic period began after 6000 BC, followed by the Bronze Age by 800 BC, and the Iron Age around 400 BC. The history of human activity in Kore such as Rice cultivation began before 3,000 B.C. as shown by the remains in **IRRI's** exhibition room.However beginning of the Korean history is often dated to 2,333 BC. Some 4,400 years ago, Altaic peoples migrated down into the Korean peninsula, with the Bronze Age Culture. These people intermingled with the natives of the peninsula to begin the development of ancient kingdoms a little before the Christian era.

Koguryo, Paekche and Shilla were the most powerful and flourishing among others. These Kingdoms rose up to occupy the whole Korean peninsula and much of Manchuria, giving the Three Kingdoms Period (57BC.-AD.668), its name.Shilla ultimately defeated her two rivals collaboratively with Tang in 668, and unified the peninsula for the first time in 676AD. As a result,Tang occupied the most part of Koguryo. During the unified Shilla Period (AD. 676-935), the peninsula experienced a cultural golden age, especially in Buddhist art.

In the succeeding Koryo Dynasty (AD. 918-1392), Korea established an aristocratic ruling government. Buddhism was the state religion and greatly influenced politics and administration. Itis interesting to note that the name"Korea"is derived from the name "Koryo".

The Choson Dynasty (1392-1910), Korea's last, adopted Confucianism as the state ideology andinstituted political and economic reforms. Among a number of important cultural developments, a surge of creative literary activities was most notable, which included the invention of the Korean alphabet, **Han-gul**, in 1443. Its capital, Hanyang, established in 1394, is now present-day Seoul, where palaces and gates from this period can still be found.When the Japanese invaded Koreain1592, the unprepared and outnumbered Korean army was driven back far into the north within several months. Fortunately, the Korean navy, headed by Admiral Yi, saved the Korea from complete collapse.The Japanese defeat at sea deprived them of a supply route in the far north, and discouraged further at tempts at invasion. This strategy of cutting supply lines prevented the Japanese invasion of China through Korea.

The Triumph of Hansan Baywas indeed one of the greatest naval conflicts ever. In the battle, Admiral Yi, used the world's first iron-clad ships, built in the form of turtle. Yi Shun-shin, as a military leader, had a rare gift for developing strategy and faithful respect for duty to his country.

The Choson Dynasty ended in 1910 and Korea was under the colonial rule of Japan until August15,1945, when Japan surrendered to the Allied Forces.Japan harshly exploited all resources in Korea and even killed millions of lives Korea.

The country was liberated, however, divided into democratic South Korea and Communist NorthKorea. Three years later, the government of the Republic of Korea was established in the South.On June25[th], 1950 with the invasion ofNorth Korea, The War : **6.25** broke out and lasted 3years until an armistice agreement was signed in 1953. After the war,South Korea made vigorous efforts to reconstruct the nation toward prosperity and stability. It achieved remarkable economic growth and became a model of developing countries. The followings are abstracts of Korean history, selected institutions and events in the history(Wikipedia)

BC 2333   King Tan-gun established Choson, Period of tribal states
BC 39~668   Koguryo
BC 18~660   Paekche Period of 3 kingdoms
BC 57~935   Shilla
918~1392   Koryo Kingdom
1392~1910   Choson Dynasty

1910~1945	Japanese colonial period, Korean refuge government in China
1945~1948	Under USA
1948~	Republic of Korea
BC 41	The King of Shilla traveled to encourage agriculture and sericulture
BC~5	The King of Pache traveled to encourage agriculture
AD~16	The King of Shilla relieved the starved
32	Princesses of Shilla led Weaving Contest
33	Rice farming begun at Paekche, the King relieved famine brought by drought
194	Koguryo established Jin-Dae-Bub (Social welfare law for the disease, widow and widower, the old and lonely, the poor)
755	Shilla commanded for filial deeds
918	Koryo established Hukchang (a social welfare fund system)
1053	Land grades are classified
1144	Recommendations for planting trees according to soils were provided
1159	Feeding standard for animals was established
1440	Bluviometer was facilitated
1446	King Sejong the great, developed Hangul, the Korean Alphabet.
1592-1598	Japanese invasion
1565	Park, Kyu-Chong and IM, Ho establish village Gye (credit union)
1729	Forbid the cut-and-burn- system above hillside
1833	Sold rice in lower price for the starved
1883	Issued Hansung Soonbo (the first newspaper)
1884	Opened the Post Office
1885	Established Paejae School
1903	Established Seoul YMCA
1906	Established the Agricultural Demonstration Station (former Rural Development Administration)
1910	Japan colonized Korea
1945	Became free from Japanese oppression and exploitation, divided into North and South Korea by the Soviet Union and United States of America
1948	Established the Republic of Korea
1950	Begun land reform, Korean War emerged (~1953)
1960, 4.19	Revolution
1961, 5.16	Coup de etat
1962	The First Economic Development Plan
1970	Saemaul Undong started
1980	Enacted Fund Law Fostering Farmers
1983	Proclaimed Rural Income Boosting Law

1988	Seoul Olympics held
1991	Strengthened Autonomous of Regional Government
1996	Enacted Law Accelerating Informationization
2002	The World Cup held

2). Land, People and Language

The Korean peninsula extends southward from the eastern end of the Asian continent. The peninsula is one of the most mountainous regions in the world, endowing the country with beautiful scenery. Hills and scenic mountains extend down the whole length of the east coast and cover about 70 percent of the land. The solid granite and limestone base of the land is lifted and folded into magnificent mountains. However, the southern and western slopes descend gradually down to the coastal plains, which produce bulk of Korea's rice crop and other agricultural products.

Korea is roughly1,000km. long and 216km. wide at its narrowest point. The land area of the Republic of Korea isabout 99,200 sq.km. and its population is 50million(2012). Administratively, the Republic of Korea consists of nine provinces(Do); one special city, Seoul; and the five metropolitan cities of Pusan, Taegu, Inchon, Kwangju and Taejon.There are 68cities(Shi) and136counties(Gun)in the nine provinces.

At present, the Korean peninsula is separated by a Demilitarized Zone at roughly the 38th parallel:the Republic of Korea in the South and the Democratic People'sRepublic of Korea in the North .Seoul is the capital as well as the financial, political, commercial, recreational, educational, and cultural heart of the Republic of Korea, containing about 10.8 million of the nation's 50 million people.

Korea falls within the temperate zone and has four distinct seasons. Spring begins in late March or early April as the trees burst into leaves.Rainfall comes in the form of occasional drizzle from March to May.Summer in Korea is relatively hot and rainy, and the vegetation is very lush. In June, the temperatures rise above 20°Celsius, and at the end of June the monsoon rains usually begin. Rainfall is heaviest in July. Autumn is rather short and lasts from the end of September to November. The air blows in from the continent bringing clear, dry weather. With the golden and red hues of the autumn foliage, this is the most pleasant season in the year with harvest of crops including rice.The winter weather is cold and dry from December to February, though spells of cold weather normally alternate with days of warmer weather. There is occasional rain or snow during this season.

The Koreans, whose ancestors used to live in northeastern Asia, mostly inManchuria and the Korean peninsula. Koreans belong to the Mongolian race, but for centuries the people have maintained their own unique language, culture and customs.The Korean language belongs to the Ural-Altaic language group, which also includes such languages as Mongolian, Hungarian, and Finnish. The Korean alphabet, called **Han-gul**was invented in 1446 by a group of scholars under the patronage of King Sejong.One of the greatestking of the Choson Dynasty is KingSejong, the fourth monarch. King Sejong, the wisest and the most humane of all monarch in Korean history, wished to give his people an easy and convenient means of communication.The King, together with the **Giphyonjon**(TheRoyalAcademy) scholars, invented the Korean Alphabet,**Hangul** which consisted of 24 letters. (Wikipedia)

3). CIs of Korean Culture

The traditional dress **Hanbok** and nine other images have been officially confirmed as " Corporate Identities " (CIs), representing KoreaorKoreanculture.ThetenareHanbok, the Korean alphabet **Hangul**, the food items "**Kimchi and pulgogi**", the Shilla Buddhist temple and grotto **Pulguk-sa** and **Sokkuram**, "**Chongmyo-jereak**" the royal ceremonial music, the Korean martial art "**Taekwondo**", **Korean Ginseng**,"**Talchum**" mask dance, **Mt. Sorak** and **world-renowned Korean born concert Musicians.**
What the officials of the Ministry of Culture and Tourism called "auxiliary" CIs will be used as images to promote Koreaabroad."*Samul-nori*" was given a special regard, as the musical performance form with the dynamic rhythm is already well known in foreign countries as a popular **Korean art.** "Sonbi-munhwa " represented the civic ethics, (Sonbi:Scholar, Munhwa: Culture, Sonbi-munhwaisymbolized by Sonbispirit which is humble, pursuing study and realization of socialjustice. Korean use as the opposite concept of Japanese Samurai.) The back court garden of Changdok Palace in Seoul was recommended as a quintessential example of Korean landscape architecture, emphasizing the beauty created by the harmony of nature, human beings and space.

2. Forerunners of Saemaul Undong

1). Patriot Yun Bong-Gil

Rural Korea in the 1920s and Shiryang-ri

Economic depression in the Korea was the most engrossing problem plaguing Koreans. The depression was due to the loss of land by the Koreans resulting from the Cadastral Survey(1910-1918) by the Japanese. The Korean farmer had steadily lost his farmland to face the throes of severe depression because of the Japanese exploiting policy.
For eleven years (1915-1926), the proportion of the landless tenant-farmers had risen to 25%. In this period, pure tenant rose from 36% to 43.8%

of the total numbers of Korean farmers. The lessees' actual net share was 17% of the product. Of the total farmers, 48.3% faced a spring shortage in food. The taxes in incomes were considerable, in view of the ratio between Koreans and Japanese in Korea. The average tax of a Korean family was 15.283yen, just 40% of the average household tax on the Japanese.It is common that the standard wages on Koreans were equivalent to 1/2~1/4 of Japanese wages. Such a condition was by no means exceptional in any part of the country during the Japanese colonial period.

Shiryang-ri, Yun's paternal home is situated in Yesan, about 160 km. South of Seoul. Shiryang-ri was situated around a crossing where many packmen passed in 1920s. The population of the village in the 1920s was 240 of 32 families. The villagers were mostly small holders and more than half of them had no titles. It is not surprising that the average size of farm land per household at Shiryang-ri was 0.56 ha.As can be seen in Table 1, the villagers suffered a severe bottle neck in their economic life. Only 4 of 23 farm households held more than 1 ha. of paddy field. Although all the farmers of the village cultivated dry fields growing vegetables and minor grains, this was only enough for their own consumption.

Table 1. Occupations and farm households by type of ownership

Categories	Agriculture			Non-agriculture		
	Proprietor	Proprietor & Tenant	Pure Tenant	Lab'r.	Others	Total
Number of Households	11	1	11	4	5	32
land/farm (ha)*	0.66	0.53	0.46	-	-	-

* Paddy Field

Patriot Yun's Life and Fellows

As is shown in Table 2, it is well known that Yun's short span of life was full of devotion to studies, dedication to the rural poor, and supreme sacrifice for the independence of his mother land. For some 13 years he studied mainly Chinese classics, ran an Evening School for the rural illiterate for the four years, organized a Reading Club and Woljin-Hoe, and setup Puheung-Won and a Consumer's CooperativeSociety.

He pursued a Utopia in his village through his Rural Rehabilitation Movement (RRM) by motivating his villagers. But there was no room for such Utopian humanitarian as Yun under Japanese rule.

After seeking political asylum in China, he killed several Japanese high ranking officers including General Shibarakawa at the ceremony for their emperor's birthday celebration in Shanghai and was executed at Osaka.

He himself was not only a patriot but at the same time also a poet, sportsman, social educator, planner and practitioner. PatriotYun had the luck to get his fellow thinkers in RRM. In spite of limited resources in his village, he mobilized them to pursue his idea. He had several young fellows who were highly educated in the village.

Table 2. Brief history of Yun the patriot

Year Age Brief Sketch
1908 Born at Shiryang-ri, Duksan-Myon, Yesan-Gun
1913 6 Begun to study Chinese Classics
1918 11 Entered Duksan Public Primary School
1919 12 Withdrew from the School, trained apiculture
1921 14 Studied Chinese Classics at Ochi-seosuk
1922 15 Got married
1926 19 Finished studies at Ochi-seosuk. Begun Evening School and RRM
1927 20 Wrote Nongmin-Dokbon
1928 21 Set up Puhueng-Won (Rehabilitation Center)
1929 22 Organized Woljin-Hoe
1930 23 Exiled to China
1932 25 Killed Japanese General, Shibarakawa at Hongkou Park, Executed

Brief sketches on some of them are as follows:
- Yun, Soon-Ui: Yun's cousin and adviser of Woljin-Hoe, studied Chinese classics.
- Yun, Shin-Deok: Yun, Soon-Ui's brother, nationalist was expelled from Joongdong Middle School because of anti-Japanese movement.
- Yun, Se-Hee: a graduate from Paejae High School took part in teaching at Evening School.
- Cheong, Jong-Gap: a graduate of Kongju Yongmyong School, Woljin-Hoe director, subscriber to a daily newspaper.
- Cheong, Jong-Ho: Brother of Cheong, Jong-Gap, Woljin-Hoe director, student of Yesan Public Agricultural High School, expelled from the school because he led an anti-Japanese movement at the school in 1931.
- Whang, Jong-Jin: Student of Yesan Public Agricultural High School, Yun's sworn brother and member of Woljin-Hoe, graduated from the school in 1931 with top prize, later became a high school principal.

Yun's Thoughts in Nongmin-Dokbon

Yun's thoughts are well expressed in his own writings, **Nongmin-**

Dokbon(Farmer'sText). Of the 3 volumes of **Nongmin-Dokbon,** the first volume and latter part of the third volume are missing. Nevertheless, what remains is enough to figure out his practical idea as shown in Table3. He emphasized harmonious personal relations in his text, and tried to develop in his studies desire for achievement, motivation, and awareness. Volume3 expresses the highlights of his ideas in terms of a physiocratical Utopia.

Table 3. Highlights of Nongmin-Dokbon

Volume II : Enlightening Part
Lesson Theme Conception
II-1 Greetings Harmonious personal relations
II-2 Proverbs Culture
II-3 Letter Harmonious personal relations
II-4 Ambition of Hero Achievement of Motivation
II-5 Don't Lose Heart Achievement of Motivation
II-6 Baek-Du Love one's native place, have patriotism and be independent
II-7 Map of Cho-Sun Love one's native place, have patriotism be independent
I -8 Wonderful World Social Adaptation
Volume III : Future of Farmer
III-1 Farmer and Laborer Equality, public welfare
III-2 Nobility and Farmer Equality
III-3 Liberty Liberalism
III-4 Farmer Physiocracy
III-5 Salt and Sugar Food processing, Marketing
III-6 Farmer and Cooperative Cooperative Spirit, Marketing Spirit Patriotism, independence
III-7 Lincoln's Study Achievement Motivation

RRM in the Aspect of RSM

A comparison of the RRM with the Rural Saemaul Movement (RSM), shows there are many similarities between them. It can be seen that most of the projects in the RRM have counterparts in the RSM as shown in Table 4.
In addition, the methods employed are also similar to those of Silhak School(**Silhak**: Korean pragmatism)and CBIRD (Community-Based Integrated Rural Development)

- It is natural that Yun had studiedChinese classics, since before and after 1910 patriotic enlightening movements were mostly initiated by scholars of Chinese classics.
- Yun's idea is based on liberalism, equality, independence, a pioneer and

cooperative spirit or realization of a physiocratical Utopia.

Table 4. RRM and RSM

RSM	RSM
‑ EveningSchool	‑ Saemaul Education
‑ Reading Club	‑ Village Library
‑ Woljin‑hoe	‑ Village Development Committee
‑ Puhueng‑won	‑ SaemaulCenter
‑MutualFinancing Association Projects For Swine Farming	‑ Income Boosting
‑ Sweet Potato Projects	‑ Food Yield Increase
‑ Cooperative Planting	‑ Cooperative Working
‑ Shu‑am‑Sports Club	‑ Saemaul Athletics
‑ Consumer's Cooperative Society	‑ Cooperative:Saemaul Kumgo

- The main project of the RRM was the Evening School, a Reading Club, Woljin‑Hoe, Puheung‑Won, a Mutual Financing Association for Swine Farming, Sweet Potato Cultivation, Cooperative Planting, the Suam‑Sports Club and a Consumer's Cooperative Society.
- Yun started with the crusade against illiteracy and then expanded the RRM to the level of self‑awareness through mobilized group activities with all young educated elites of the village.
- In development of theory, the thoughts pursued in the RRM are in the same stream with the spirit of the Silhak School, RSM and CBIRD.
- Most references about Yun are concerned with his heroic deed in Shanghai. A similar tendency is found in the students' images of him. However, Patriot Yun is a typical community organizer, or in other words, a forerunner of Saemaul Undong.

2). Elder Kim Yong‑Ki and Canaan Farmers' School

Elder Kim's Life and Canaan Farmers' School

Elder Kim Yong‑Ki was born on September 5, 1912 at Nungnaeri Wabu Myon, Yangju Kun, Kyonggido, Korea. When he was 3 years old his father became a Christian, and he was greatly moved by the Bible and he became a Christian elder later. In November 1945, Kim Yong‑Ki, a deacon of a church then, came to Poong San Ri, Dong Boo Myon, Kwang Joo Kun, Kyonggido, this is the place where the first Farmers' School was established. Elder Kim is the man who began farming on infertile soil when he reached the age 20, and he repeated this kind of venture in several places and has made a fertile farm land out of them, changing each at ten-year intervals. This particular place of Poong San Ri is the fourth one that he had started. His family consisted of his wife, 3 sons and 2 daughters. Then he purchased an uncultivated low mountain measuring 10,000 pyong (3.3 ha.), lived in a tent and started cultivating it. Elder Kim recalls the original mountain as follows in his book entitled, The Road to Canaan. "The soil was completely acid, therefore, vegetable, grass and trees couldn't grow - I decided to start cultivating the soil to make a model out of this kind of infertile land". He assembled people and he gave his lecture to the audience. His slogan was "Don't be a man to command, but be a man standing to his own". He spoke eloquently about his experiences of having cultivated infertile soil. His lecture was neither based on any theory nor academic thesis. It was based on his real experience which impress farmers. The lectures given by him with the help of his children became the backbone of the Canaan Farm spirit of the day.The Canaan Farmers' School was opened in 1954 in an effort to spread Christianity to the rural villages and communities of the country. The effort was initiated in early 1933 as reclamation movement for the building of an ideal village. The school was located in eastern suburbs of Seoul. In 1962 the first session of education was begun at the request of the villagers with 42 young male and female farmers. Twenty years later, another Canaan Farmers' School was additionally created in Wonsong-gun, Kangwon-do and has provided social education to rural leaders, various workers, and soldiers. In August 1966, Elder Kim Yong-Ki received the **Magsaysay Award**(Social Service Award), and because of this, the Canaan Farmers' School became more famous. His life is introduced in Table 5.

Table 5. Elder Kim's Life

1909	Born in Sept. 5 at Bongan-chon, Neungnae-ri, Choan-myon, Namyang-gun, Kyonggi-do,Korea.
1931	Established Bongan Ideal Village.
1944	Organized farmers' union and Independence Movement
1962	Established the First CanaanFarmers'School.
1966	Awarded Magsaysay Prize.
1973	Established the Second Canaan Farmers' School, Awarded the First InchonCulturalPrize.
1978	Received the Honorary Degree of Doctor of Humanity at XavierUniversity,Philippines.
1988	Passed away on August 1 at his home in Pungsan-dong, HanamCity,Kyonggi-do,Korea.

Training and Guidelines

The training at the school originally proceeded in three stages:
(1) 15 days for spiritual training, (2) 15 days for the practice of farming skills and (3) 15 days of leadership. This schedule has been shortened so that an average of six-to-seven sessions of training are carried out in a year.
His detailed guidelines selected for people are as follows:

Economical life
- Use domestic products
- Don't waste tooth paste, soap, water, and energy
- Wear simple and practical clothes and shoes
- Don't eat between meals and don't visit coffee shops so often
- Read book during leisure hours
- Don't make a fancy hair-do
- Try to make use of waste materials
- Don't gamble
- Don't hold luxurious wedding ceremonies
- Don't hold luxurious funeral services
- Don't hold luxurious ritual ceremonies for the deceased

Family life
- Early rising and early sleeping
- Treat friend like oneself
- Everyone in the family helps in cleaning
- The children are supposed to let the parents know before they leave the house
- Try to economize spending money and save for special gifts for parents
- Don't complain
- Marry with parents' consent
- Brothers respect other's opinion
- No divorce except with church's approval
- Husband and wife keep their fidelity
- Wife shouldn't be bossy
- Respect parents-in-law
- Love daughter-in-law
- Treat house guests well
- Read books at least an hour a day

Social life
- Don't cut a line when waiting
- Make room for others in the bus

- Don't spit and don't throw garbage on the street
- Keep the public toilet clean
- Don't forget to greet people
- Don't be late for appointments and keep your promises
- Use good words
- Respect seniors and assist the handicaps in walking.

The school's basic ideologies and philosophy in order to conquer the deeply-rooted poverty of rural society, it is inevitable to have farmers as the "fourth army" who are equipped with Christianity with which to drive any psychological and material poverty.The objectives of the school are : (1) to strengthen national citizenship, (2) to practice ways of life for desirable national ethics and norms, (3) to enhance democratic leadership (4) to establish appropriate views in terms of family, society and nation, (5) to equip people with the habits of thrift and saving, and (6) to develop capabilities to overcome poverty.

In order to achieve these objectives, the school provides the following guidelines:

- Spiritual training based on the Christian faith, to strengthen indomitable will and mental power through training moral attitude, temperate living and psychological and physical disciplines;
- Training of group life in a community sense to develop cooperation and self-controlling character in order to achieve public welfare individually and in society through autonomous group activities in a life of mutual rooming and boarding in the dormitories;
- Training for the whole man to develop a "whole man" who is balanced in life, knowledge and behavior as one individual with character through encounters with the whole characters of the trainees.
- Training for adult leaders to train capable social leaders for those who have completed their regular education through helping them adjust to rapid social changes, and encouraging them to build new vision, practice with the vision and adjust to rapid social development.

The 1ˢᵗCanaan Farmers School in Hanam City, Korea

The Training Effectiveness

One of the characteristics of the school curriculum is that there is no subject related to Christian religion at all since the training is assumed to enhance desirable ways of thinking and practices through emphasis on life experiences themselves. This has been a good point for those who have once completed the training. Because of this voluntary application procedure, the training effectiveness is recognized to be high. In fact, it is true that a number of procedures and techniques of today's SaemaulEducation have been adopted from the Canaan Farmers' Schoolprograms. Jogging in the early morning and living together in dormitories are two examples of these. The government has approved the school a Saemaul Education Institute and has encouraged young people to receive training at the school.During the 30 years of its history, about 500 thousand people have completed the Canaan School training and are trying to live according to what they have learned at the school in various working places or rural villages. They also continue to recommend new applicants for the school training. This seems to be kept continuously by the conviction that their experiences at the school are valuable and necessary for their daily lives. In this sense, the Canaan School must certainly have contributed to the enhancement of a sound social atmosphere and the sense of fellowship of people. This contribution is recognized in and out of the country and Elder Kim has been awarded various prizes and public commendations.

How this kind of social education institution could have continued to exist as a civilian organization without any financial assistance from the government, especially as a **SaemaulEducation Institute**since 1972. In response, the school has operated without difficulties through charging trainees for necessary expenses under a principle of "paying in beneficiary's responsibility". There is, thus, an advantage in that the school need not respond to any pressure from authorities who would have tended to exercise an influence because of their assistance. Even in applying their "principle of beneficiary's payment", the school operates with flexibility through imposing more expenses upon those who attend by request of the government or firms for the education than those voluntarily participating farmers and students. In one sense, "principle of beneficiary's payment"also stimulates trainees to seek positive benefits and, thus, become more effective than when given free tuition.

The Canaan Farmers' School has contributed to spread a sound social value through its training methods and the principle of "paying in beneficiary's responsibility ".

Il-Ga Award for the Realization of Bokminism

Bokminism is a new idea grown out of farm youth's anti-Japanese national resistance movement to stand against the Japanese harsh National Liquidation Policy in 1930s. The idea which practices wasteland reclamation, church renovation, national consciousness and life revolutionary movement is to prevent poverty and establish a righteous society by the teachings of the Bible. It also aims to establish the national community passing over all their ideologies such as Capitalism or Communism to lead the nation of sixty million to Canaan,"the land of milk and honey".

The IGMAF (Il-Ga Memorial Award Foundation)

The foundation was established in honor of Dr. Yong-ki, Kim (Il-Ga is the pen name of Elder Yong-ki, Kim), on September 5, 1989. People who have the same goal as Elder Yong-ki, Kim desiring to succeed and develop the spirit of Bokminism came together and proposed to initiate the Il-Ga Award system.The Il-Ga Award does not only mean to give hope and courage to those who are underprivileged and praise Il-Ga's passionate pioneering spirit but also to pay a high tribute to the unrecognized workers who have dedicated themselves to helping others. The IGMAF will continue to support the development of a social movement which is based on the ideology of Bokminism so as to ensure that love and justice may prosper on this land. Table 6 shows selected winners of Il-Ga Prize and the Prize has been conducted every year.

Oversea's Canaan Farmers' School

For international sharing of experiences and diffusion of Bokminism, the Canaan Farmers' School laid the cornerstone of Canaan Farmers' Training Center, in the province of Bataan, Philippines on June 6, 1997. .

Currently, the number of oversea's Canaan Farmers' School is increasing.

Since Bangladesh Canaan Famers' School was founded in 1991, lots of Canaan Farmers' Schools has been founded in the Philippines, Myanmar, China, Indonesia, Jordan, India, and Thailand. Besides those countries, more Canaan Farmers' Schools are under preparation for establishment in Ghana, Palestine, Laos, Malawi, Malaysia, Cambodia, Uzbekistan and Uganda in the future.

II. Cooperative Heritages and Agricultural Extension

1.Mutual Aid and Seed Money

Collecting seed money is very important for both individual and community aspects as well. For this, many Koreans have participated in various Gyes (a private loan association: **Kumgo**), since several centuries ago. A Gye is much beyond mere accumulation of money because it enhances friendship of members and provides mutual assistance for the community where it belongs. There are various Gyes such as:

-Village Gye,
-Relative Gye,
-Alumni Gye,
-Same Age Group Gye,
-Colleague Gye and so on.

Many Koreans organized such Gyes even abroad where they migrated. Usually the period of any Gye is one to several years and some continued for several hundred years. The origin of Gye is unknown. However, there are several Gyes established hundreds of years ago which have continued up to now.

In 1565, villagers of Gurim-Ri, Gunso Myon, Yong Am Gum, Cholla-nam Do, organized a village Gye. Park, Kyu Chong and Im-Ho led and organized it through collecting rice among members.

Major activities:
- Mutual support in marriage and burial
- Protection of forestry (prohibit deforestation)
- Extended help to non-members in the community
- Improvement and maintenance of roads and bridges
- Cleanliness of village
- Prevention of demoralization

The Gye established primary school in 1907, which was three years prior to Japanese colonization of Korea (1910). After 1945, the villagers led the government to establish Gurim Middle School and Gurim High School through donation of seed money. Presently, there are dozens of villagers enrolled in the Gye and their own building.

In 1629, villagers of Kyongsan village, Burim-Myon, Euryong Kun, Kyong Sang NamDo, established autonomous regulations and rules for their villagers and membership criteria of Village Gye. The rules and regulations contain the following:

- Mutual regulation upon mistakes and crime
- Mutual aid upon marriage and burial or disaster
- Membership criteria of village Gye

Korea's Historical Context to the Saemaul Kumgo

Viewed from the aims and objectives of the on-going Saemaul Undong and its emphasis on people's cooperation, the Saemaul Undong has been readily accepted to have the same context as that of the Korean traditional cooperative activity, which is deeply-rooted in Pumasi(exchange of farm labor), Dure(farmers' field cooperative work), Gye(a private loan association) and Hyangyak(a written village code). The movement geared towards building ideal villages was spearheaded earlier in Korea by Korea's noted educator, the late Anh Chang-Ho (penname-Tosan). This campaign can be said to be the present pattern of the prevailing Saemaul Undong. Ahn Chang-Ho advocated this movement for the creation of ideal villages with the aim of preserving the homogeneity of Korean people and of improving people's prosperity through proper utilization of resources and technical know-how available in regional communities and by people cooperative efforts. Anh Chang-Ho, thus, stressed the comprehensive socio-economic development of regional communities. Such characteristics of the movement which is the creation of ideal villages are almost tantamount to that of the present Saemaul Undong. From a modern sense, the present patterns of the on-going Saemaul Undong can be said to be represented by regional community development projects undertaken earlier in the 1950's and the subsequent People's Movement for National Reconstruction carried out in the 1960s.Launching of Saemaul Kumgo Activity and its Developmental Progress. The historical context of Saemaul Kumgo on activity can also be traced back to Pumasi, dure,Gyeand Hyangyakwhich prevailed in ancient times in Korea. As a matter of fact, the firstSaemaul Kumgo established in 1963 is said to be the cradle of the present Saemaul credit union activity in the Republic of Korea. In1964, thenumber of Saemaul Kumgo increased to 60 nationwide. In keeping pace with the steady promotion of the Saemaul Undong,the expansion of the Saemaul Kumgo activity was adopted in 1972 as a priority program within the framework of Saemaul Kumgo. It was formally established in Seoul on March 22, 1973 under the umbrella of the Headquarters of Saemaul Undong.In 1979, the number of Saemaul Kumgos made sharp increase, thus bringing the total number ofSaemaul Kumgos to 39,625.

2. Community Credit Cooperatives

Community Credit Cooperatives(CCC : Saemaul Kumgo) is a small thrift institution based on its own and neighboring communities. Apart from credit unions of a same origin, community credit cooperatives have been under the jurisdiction of the Ministry of Security and Public Administration.

History

A community credit cooperative originated with a village credit union established in Hadun-Ri, Saengcho-Myun, Saancheong-Kun, South Gyeongsang Province in May 25, 1963 under the auspices of the National Reconstruction Movement Federation ..

Following the 1972 implementation of the Credit Unions Act, community credit cooperatives fell under the provisions of that act and the nomenclature for them was unified as "village banks".

Upon 1982 enactment of the Community Credit Cooperatives Act,the name was then changed to "community credit cooperatives", and a solid foundation was laid for the independent development of community credit cooperatives.

Business and Services

A community credit cooperative provides the following services:

- receipt of deposits and installment deposits from members,
- extension of loans to members, domestic exchange services;
- execution of business on behalf of the government, public organizations or financial institutions; and
- separate safekeeping, and so on.

Except for certain services such as the discounting of bills, a community credit cooperative performs nearly the same functions as a credit union

Regarding operational restrictions, a community credit cooperative is only allowed to borrow funds from the Korean Federation of Community Credit Cooperatives, the government, public organizations or financial institutions, within the limits of the aggregate of its invested capital and reserved funds.

Its credit ceilings on individual borrowers may not exceed 20 percent of the aggregate of its invested capital and reserved funds. It must also maintain a minimum of 10 percent of the balance of its deposits and installment deposits as repayment reserves, and must deposit half of those reserves with the Korean Federation of Community Credit Cooperatives.

Nationwide Organization

The Korean Federation of Community Credit Cooperatives, a non-profit corporate body composed of community credit cooperatives, deals in the following services:

- guidance on, surveys of and training in the businesses of member cooperatives;
- inspection and supervision of member cooperatives;
- provision of mutual aid services; and
- conduct of projects commissioned to it by the government or public organizations.

It also provides the following services:

- receipts of deposits and installment deposits from member cooperatives;
- lending of funds, guarantees of payments, and discounts of bills for members;
- domestic and foreign exchange services;
- separate safekeeping;
- execution of business on behalf of the government, public organizations or financial institutions; and
- the underwriting and sale of securities; and
- deposit protection reserve fund to guarantee the return of deposits and other savings to members.

Statistics

By the time the Community Credit Cooperatives Act was legislated there were 11,719 community credit cooperatives in operation, with combined membership of 5.38 million.

However, the implementation of this act was followed by a reorganization of insolvent cooperatives, causing the total members of cooperatives and their members to decline sharply — to 5,360 and 3.84 million, respectively, by the end of 1983. The number of cooperatives has continued to decrease in the period since, while membership has gradually increased. As of end-June 2011 there were 1,466 cooperatives in operation, engaging in transactions with 15.97 million members.

As of end-June 2011, community credit cooperatives secured up to 87.5 percent of their total funds from deposits including installment deposits, and allocated these funds among loans (53.0 percent), cash and deposits (25.2

Status of Saemaul Kumgo's Activity

Saemaul Kumgo's activity during the 1980s put an end to its mere quantitative expansion in past decades. Instead, Saemaul Kumgo's has concentrated its endeavors on the gradual renovation of its institutional mechanism in an effort to enhance its public confidence in conjunction with the rationalization of its operations. Presently, Saemaul Kumgos are increasingly taking root among urban and rural people to serve as a centripetal force for the creation and allocation of capital by "meager grass roots people," and for the "grassroots' people" themselves in regional communities.In line with the ever-increasing urbanization trend in this country, the socio-economic characteristics of urban cities and rural communities are reshaping as time goes by. Not only individuals but also organizational institutions are mandated to cope sagaciously with this societal transformation. Saemaul Kumgos are no exceptions to this principal rule of action. From this point of view, there must be no question but we must look at the influence of existing Saemaul Kumgos for regional community development, the present status by regional area, for patterns and developmental indicators and future developmental orientation.

As of January 1, 1983, the law governing the operation of Saemaul Kumgos was legally instituted and promulgated. Under the legal provisions, a deposit insurance system for the safety of Kumgo members and in solvent Kumgos were merged into other Kumgos, thus rationalizing the operations of Saemaul Kumgo activity. As a result, by the end of 1985, the number of Saemaul Kumgos decreased to 4,174. However, the total assets of these Saemaul Kumgos made a remarkable increase.Under the Saemaul Kumgo activity, both large and small have placed an emphasis on publishing Saemaul Kumgo activity to the public through a thorough in-service training of executive directors and staff.The majority of respondents from both successful and small credit unions favored a kind attitude to their clients, according to the highest proportion of those questioned.Preferential medical treatment has been given to some members of Saemaul Kumgos; however, the ratio of the number of household Saemaul Kumgos giving such preferential medical treatment to their members was very low, in general.Ninety-one percent of successful Saemaul Kumgos and 56 percent of the small ones have been estimated to have contributed greatly themselves to eliminate usurious loans borrowed by poor rural people.As factors for the promotion of the activity in the case of successful Saemaul Kumgos, a high moral influence and financial capability of executive members and the guiding principles of those unions putting an emphasis on the increase of profits and welfare of their memberships were indicated. Meanwhile, in the case of the small Saemaul Kumgos, backwardness was indicated to have stemmed from unsatisfactory publicity of their meritorious activity to the public for the most part.All executive directors of Saemaul Kumgo foresee that Saemaul credit union activity would be promoted in year 2000s.

Successful Saemaul Kumgos are expected to make more substantial growth than the small ones.In farming villages, too, the difference between successful Saemaul Kumgos and the small ones has been similar to that noted in urban cities. However, in general, Saemaul Kumgos operating in farming villages showed somewhat lower expectation for their promotional activity in 2000s, than that of urban areas. Such a difference noted between urban area and those in farming villages and between those of successful unions and small ones are judged to have resulted from their geographical situation, that is, people's economic capability.

As of the end of August 1985 the ratio of the number of Saemaul Kumgo membership to the total population of Korea stood at 9.5 percent. The ratio of the number of members of Saemaul Kumgos to population in urban cities was 14%. As of the end of 1995, a comparison of Saemaul Kumgo and selected cooperatives is shown in Table 6.

Table 6 .Selected Cooperatives and Saemaul Kumgo (1995)

Cooperatives	No. of Cooperatives	No. of Members (1,000)	No. of Employees	Funds (100million won)	Vol of Business (100 million won)
Agri-Cooperatives	1.401	2,010	70,179	23,517	1,108.825
Credit Union	1,678	4,339	12,675	26,988	140,966
Saemaul Kumgo	2,931	10,408	20,344	31,939	271,933

Source: Korean Federation of Community Credit Cooperatives (Korean Federation of Saemaul Kumgos), National Agricultural Cooperative Federation.

Saemaul Kumgo and the Nationwide Network of Saemaul Undong

Saemaul Kumgo activity is based on people's self-support cooperative organizations, which is deeply rooted in Korea's traditional cooperative spirit. The Saemaul Kumgo activity is to raise necessary funds by the members themselves. This activity makes good use of accumulated funds for the benefit of members themselves and thus, enhances the socio-economic and cultural standards of people in their daily lives. This activity will eventually strengthen people's spiritual posture and national economic development through regional community development activities.

The substantial nature of such aims and objectives of Saemaul Kumgo activity is explicitly manifested in the provisions of Article 1 of the Law governing Saemaul Kumgo activity. Article 1 of the law stipulates that "Saemaul Kumgo activity aims at creating funds by the people of the same regional community and assuring that profits accruing from that activity would be fed-back to the people of the relevant regional community themselves".Saemaul Kumgos served as centers for the welfare of the people of a regional community. They not only arouse the spirit among regional people to lead frugal lives but also served as an organ to help poor people become self-reliant. Moreover, they contribute themselves to the regional community development by providing support funds out of their profits for the successful performance of Saemaul projects.

Layout of Saemaul Kumgo in Regional Communities

In the case of Saemaul Kumgo operating in farming villages, though there are some differences resulting from peculiarities of the community concerned, the Saemaul Kumgo is encouraged to be set up by a primary school district for the most part. Thus, there are many **MyonorEup**(lower echelon administrative units) which have one or more Saemaul Kumgos.In the case of urban cities, one Saemaul Kumgo operates per **Dong**(Lower echelon administrative unit) on the average.

The Federation of Saemaul Kumgo, after it was established as a member organization of the Headquarters of Saemaul Undong, developed a campaign to allow each family have a bank book per household to enhance thrift and economy in their daily lives. This campaign has attained considerable achievement. According to provisions specified in paragraph 4 of Article 8 of the Implementing Regulations of the Law governing the operation of Saemaul Kumgo activity, each and every Saemaul Kumgo has been providing less than one hundred of their profits as support funds for successful performance of Saemaul projects. It is foreseeable that the amount of such support funds would be increased with ever-growing Saemaul Kumgo activity.

The present status of Saemaul Kumgos by regional community, of patterns, and set of developmental indicators and the connection of Saemaul Kumgo activity to the nationwide network of Saemaul Undong, the following conclusion have been derived:

First, after 1980 insolvent Saemaul Kumgos were realigned and subsequent Saemaul Kumgos ' successful operations for the most part, thereby contributing to the community development, have been pursued.

Second, a difference between Saemaul Kumgos operating in urban cities and those active in farming villages, and a parity between successful Saemaul Kumgo and small ones seemed to stem for the most part not from their different management techniques but from their geographical situation, that is, the members' economic capability.

Third, in spite of the ever-growing quantitative expansion of Saemaul Kumgos, no mechanism that is entitled to train specialists properly has been set up as yet.

Fourth, Saemaul Kumgos have been well-organized. They have contributed to the substantial promotion of the prevalent Saemaul Undong and effective cooperation among memberships. However, there is still much room for Saemaul Kumgos to assure satisfactory funds needed for successful performance of Saemaul projects in the relevant regional community.Fifth, the on-going urban Saemaul Undong would be more important than ever before in parallel with growing urbanization trend. There arises a need to intensify people's spiritual training to make people establish their cooperative posture as democratic citizens. Sixth, the ongoing international sharing movement including official development assistance (ODA) and non-government organization (NGOs) activities must be pursued steadily as a means to propagate Korea's genuine experiences of successful community development to foreign countries, especially those of developing nations based on the south-south cooperative spirit.It will judged that if and when the Saemaul Kumgo activity is to be pushed and based on this promotion effective performance of community development projects is to be expected, the following effects must be pursued actively:First, resources available in regional communities must be explored through the Saemaul Undong and each and every citizen of the regional communities must be kept informed of the fact that resultant benefits would be allocated to residents themselves. Second, in order to keep abreast with the accelerating social transformation and prospects for the year of 2000 specialist training for Saemaul Kumgo activities must be carried out. Concentrated effects must be made to train not only executive members of the staff of credit unions but also to every resident of regional communities.Third, community leaders in the area where the Saemaul Kumgos concerned are located, and other leaders affiliated with Saemaul organizations must actively take part in the promotion of Saemaul Kumgo activities. Along with individual participation in Saemaul Kumgos activity as was the case of the past, it is desirable to actively induce available funds into Saemaul Kumgos to be used as a mutual fund. To elaborate, not only one community basic fund but also inter-community common capital should be created as much as possible. Moreover, the scope of Kumgo's support for successful performance of Saemaul projects must also be expanded capable of covering inter-community Saemaul projects for more effective end-results.

Fourth, inter-flow of information between Saemaul Kumgos operations in urban cities and those active in farming villages must be effected as far as possible and their inter-operational cooperation must also be substantiated.

This work, if possible, would be favorable for the improvement of marketing of agricultural products.

Korea Federation of Community Cooperatives

 KFCC was established in 1973 to supervise the work of CC, increase joint interests, and promote sound development. As a partner of CC, it is establishing management conditions pursued by CC, helping it to achieve continued growth.

MAIN businesses

 Its main businesses include guidance and supervision, which involve supporting the management of CC for sound growth and supervising CC. As for its credit business, it is performing the role of a central bank by controlling the CC's liquidity. It also handles public relations and the insurance business for CC and its members, manages Depositors Protection Fund to guarantee the return of savings of CC members in emergencies, and is in charge of training the directors and staff of CC and KFCC. It is also engaging in domestic and foreign investigation and research for long-term development of CC and KFCC. The goal of its international cooperation business is to foster friendships and strengthen cooperation with international cooperative societies.

3. Korean Credit Union(Wikipedia)

Differences from other financial institutions

Credit unions differ from banksand other financial institutions in that those who have accounts in the credit union are its members and owners, and they elect their board of directors in aone-person-one-vote system regardless of their amount invested. Credit unions see themselves as different from mainstream banks, with a mission to be "community-oriented" and "serve people, not profit.

Credit unions offer many of the same financial services as banks, but often using a different terminology; common services include share accounts (savings accounts), share draft accounts (checking accounts), credit cards, share term certificates (certificates of deposit), and online banking.Normally, only a member of a credit union may deposit or borrowmoney. Surveys of customers at banks and credit unions have consistently shown a significantly higher customer satisfaction rate with the quality of service at credit unions.Credit unions have historically claimed to provide superior member service and to be committed to helping members improve their financial situation. In the context of financial inclusion credit unions claim to provide a broader range of loan and savings products at a much cheaper cost to their members than do most microfinance institutions.

1). Characteristics and Global Presence of Credit Union

Not-for-profit status

In the credit union context, "not-for-profit" is not the same as for a "non-profit" charity or similar organization. Credit unions are "not-for-profit" because their purpose is to serve their members rather than to maximize profits. For instance, Delta Community Credit Union is a state chartered nonprofit cooperative credit union owned by its members.But, unlike charities and the like, credit unions do not rely on donations, and are financial institutions that must perforce make what is, in economic terms, a small profit (i.e., in non-profit accounting terms, a "surplus") to remain in existence.According to the World Council of Credit Unions (WOCCU), a credit union's revenues (from loans and investments) must exceed its operating expenses and dividends (interest paid on deposits) in order to maintain capital and solvency. WOCCU's position is deeply rooted in global credit union history. F.W. Raiffeisen, the founder of the global movement, wrote in 1870 that credit unions "are, according to paragraph eleven of the German law of cooperatives, 'merchants' as defined by the common code of commerce. They accordingly form a sort of commercial business enterprise of which the owners are the Credit Unions' members".

Global Presence

Based on data from the World Council, at the end of 2010 there were 52,945 credit unions in 100 countries around the world. Collectively they served 188 million members and oversaw US$1.5 trillion in assets. The World Council does not include data from co-operative banks, so, for example, some countries generally seen as the pioneers of credit unionism, such as Germany, France, the Netherlands and Italy, are not always included in their data. The European Association of Co-operative Banks reported 38 million members in those four countries at the end of 2010.

The countries with the most credit union activity are highly diverse. According to the World Council, the countries with the greatest number of credit union members were the United States (92 million), India (20 million), Canada (11 million), South Korea (5.6 million), Kenya and Brazil (3.9 million each), Thailand (3.6 million), Australia 3.4 million, Ireland (3.0 million), and Mexico (2.6 million).

The countries with the highest percentage of credit union members in the economically active population were Ireland (75%), Barbados (72%), St. Lucia (67%), Belize (65%), Grenada (59%), Trinidad & Tobago and Jamaica (54% each), Canada (46%), Antigua & Barbuda (45%), and the United States (44%). Several African and Latin American countries also had high credit union membership rates, as did Australia. The average percentage for all countries considered in the report was 7.5%

Credit unions were launched in Poland in 1992; as of 2012 there were 2,000 credit union branches there with 2.2 million members.

History

Modern credit union history dates from 1852, when Franz Hermann Schulze-Delitzsch consolidated the learning from two pilot projects, one in Eilenburg and the other in Delitzsch in the Kingdom of Saxony into what are generally recognized as the first credit unions in the world. He went on to develop a highly successful urban credit union system. In 1864 Friedrich Wilhelm Raiffeisen founded the first rural credit union in Heddesdorf (now part of Neuwied) in Germany. By the time of Raiffeisen's death in 1888, credit unions had spread to Italy, France, the Netherlands, England, Austria, and other nations.

The first credit union in North America, the Caisse Populaire de Lévis in Quebec, Canada, began operations on January 23, 1901 with a 10-cent deposit. Founder Alphonse Desjardins, a reporter in the Canadian parliament, was moved to take up his mission in 1897 when he learned of a Montrealer who had been ordered by the court to pay nearly C$5,000 in interest on a loan of $150 from a moneylender. Drawing extensively on European precedents, Desjardins developed a unique parish-based model for Quebec: the caisse populaire.

In the United States, St. Mary's Bank Credit Union of Manchester, New Hampshire was the first credit union. Assisted by a personal visit from Desjardins, St. Mary's was founded by French-speakingimmigrants to

Manchester from Quebec on November 24, 1908. America's Credit Union Museum now occupies the location of the home from which St. Mary's Bank Credit Union first operated. On November 1910 the Woman's Educational and Industrial Union set up the Industrial Credit Union, modelled on the Desjardins credit unions it was the first non-faith-based community credit union serving all people in the greater Boston area. The oldest state wide credit union in the US was established in 1913. The St. Mary's Credit Union serves any resident of the Commonwealth of Massachusetts.

After being promoted by the Catholic Church in the 1940s to assist the poor in Latin America, credit unions expanded rapidly during the 1950s and 1960s, especially in Bolivia, Costa Rica, the Dominican Republic, Honduras and Peru. The Regional Confederation of Latin American Credit Unions (COLAC) was formed and with funding by the Inter-American Development Bank credit unions in the regions grew rapidly throughout the 1970s and into the early 1980s. In 1988 COLAC credit unions represented 4 million members across 17 countries with a loan portfolio of circa half a billion US dollars. However, from the late 1970s onwards many Latin American credit unions struggled with inflation, stagnating membership and serious loan recovery problems. In the 1980s donor agencies such as USAID attempted to rehabilitate Latin American credit unions by providing technical assistance and focusing credit unions' efforts on mobilising deposits from the local population. In 1987 the regional financial crisis caused a run on credit unions. Significant withdrawals and high default rates caused liquidity problems for many credit unions in the region.

Stability and Risks

Credit unions must make enough surplus to cover expenses, otherwise, like any other business, they cannot continue. They can and do become insolvent and cease to exist; the effect on those with funds deposited varies between jurisdictions.

Several factors combine to put credit unions at risk of failure. They may not be allowed to lend enough money to enough people who are willing and able to repay because of their rules on responsible lending. When debtors get into trouble, they will often repay liabilities such as payday loans with high interest rates first, leaving the credit unions until last. And in some cases courts may, after ruling against debtors, leniently allow them to pay off their debts with very small payments, sometimes free of interest, over a long period.

Credit unions as such provide service only to individual consumers. Corporate credit unions (also known as central credit unions in Canada) provide service to credit unions, with operational support, funds clearing tasks, and product and service delivery.

Leagues and Associations

Credit Unions often form cooperatives among themselves to provide services to members. A Credit Union Service Organization (CUSO) is generally a for-profit subsidiary of one or more credit unions formed for this purpose. For example, CO-OP Financial Services, the largest credit union owned interbank network in the US, provides an ATM network and shared branching services to credit unions. Other examples of cooperatives among credit unions include credit counseling services as well as insurance and investment services.

State credit union leagues can partner with outside organizations to promote initiatives for credit unions or customers. For example, the Indiana Credit Union League sponsors an initiative called "Ignite", which is used to encourage innovation in the credit union industry, with the Filene Research Institute.

The WCCU is both a trade association for credit unions worldwide and a development agency. The WOCCU's mission is to "assist its members and potential members to organize, expand, improve and integrate credit unions and related institutions as effective instruments for the economic and social development of all people".

Korean Credit Unions.

Korean credit union movement started in May 1960 by an American nun, Sister Mary Gabriella (1900~1993).She organized the Holy Family Credit Union and mobilized 27 members, employees of Maryknoll Hospital and Catholic Relief Services in Busan. Since Father Chang Dae-ik(1923~2008) established the Central Credit Union in June 1960, the credit union movement has extended to almost of all municipalities.Korean credit union has dedicated to the small holders by providing micro finance. (www.cu.co.kr)

Brief History of Korean Credit Unions

May
1960 "Holy Family Credit Union" was firstly established by Sr. Mary Gabriella

Jun.
1960 "Catholic central credit union" was established by Father Chang, Dae-ik

Apr. The Korea Credit Union League, a trade association was founded with
1964 63 member credit unions

May
1965 Affiliated with the CUNA International, former WOCCU

Apr.
1971 ACCU was founded in Seoul by 9 Asian countries

Aug.
1972 The Korea Credit Union Act was promulgated

Mar.
1973 NACUFOK, former KCUL was organized according to the Act

Dec. Structure was changed into three-tier system from two-tier system ;
1988 Credit Union, Provincial League, and NACUFOK

May
1998 Reached KRW20trillion total assets

Sept.
2008 Reached KRW 30 trillion total assets

Jan.
2010 Reached KRW 40 trillion total assets

Sept.
2010

Vision Declaration ceremony commemorating the 50th anniversary and
ACCU Forum & Annual General Meeting held in Seoul.

The total number of credit union, member and asset are shown in the
Table 7 Since 2001, the number of credit has been decreased. On the
contrary asset has been increased. However the number of credit has
kept around five million for the last ten years.

Table 7 General status of Credit Union in Korea in selected years

Year	2001	2006	2011
No of Credit	1,268	1,027	955
No of Member 10 thousend	537	470	586
Asset10,000millionWon	2,206	2,600	4,960

4. The National Agricultural Cooperative Federation

The National Agricultural Cooperative (NACF)was established in 1961 to enhance the social and economic status of its membership and to promote a balanced development of the national economy. Its role is divided into three areas: marketing and supply, banking and insurance, and extension services. Although literally referring to local member cooperatives, the term nonghyup is used by South Koreans to describe both a local cooperative (Korean:농협) and the NACF (Korean: 농협중앙회)(Wikipedia).

History

- 2013 - An opposition lawmaker and the media exposed NACF's unethical business practice of paying newspapers to run promo articles.
- 2012 - NACF restructured into a federation with two holding companies, to increase effectiveness and competitiveness
- 2011 - Ranked ninth largest cooperative by the International Cooperative Alliance[2]
- 2011 - Opened NH Residential Hall to accommodate 500 students from farming households
- 2011 - Launched 50th anniversary emblem and slogan
- 2008 - Ranked third largest cooperative by the International Cooperative Alliance
- 2008 - Opened International Banking(IB) center
- 2006 - Hosted the 37th World Farmers' Congress of the International Federation of Agricultural Producers (IFAP)
- 2004 - Launched the "New Rural Community and New Agricultural Cooperative" campaign
- 2004 - Established Nonghyup Culture and Welfare Foundation
- 2002 - Co-founded NH-CA Asset Management, Ltd. with the FrenchCrédit Agricole
- 2001 - Hosted the International Co-operative Alliance(ICA) General Assembly
- 2000 - Launched the integrated NACF, consolidating the federations of agricultural, livestock, and ginseng cooperatives
- 1998 - Acquired ISO 9002 certification for the NACF brand Kimchi, which was designated the official food for 1998 Olympics
- 1995 - Founded the Korea Agricultural Cooperative Marketing, Inc, a subsidiary for produce distribution and sales
- 1989 - Introduced a direct election system for the president of member cooperatives and the chairperson of the NACF
- 1986 - Began supplying tax-free oil for farm machinery and equipment

- 1981 – Restructured the 3-tier organization to a 2-tier organization, consisting of individual cooperatives and the federation
- 1961 – Established the NACF, consolidating agricultural cooperatives and the Agricultural Bankin accordance with Agricultural Cooperative Law

Member cooperatives are democratically controlled, autonomous business groups, funded by member subscriptions rather than government financial investment. They, in turn, fund the NACF through institutional subscriptions. Cooperatives are governed by directly elected presidents, who, in turn, elect a chairman of the federation.

Member farmers and associate members

Member cooperatives allow non-farmers, who have invested a certain amount of capital into the cooperative, to open tax-free bank accounts and access some services. However, whereas member farmers are defined as the genuine owners or stakeholders, associate members can only obtain limited access to or influence over the cooperative

As of December 2011, the number of the member farmers was 2,446,836 and the number of the associate members was 15,262,611. In 2010, these figures were 2,447,765 and 14,483,532, respectively, indicating a decline in member farmers of 929, and an increase in associate members of 779,079.

Table8.Number of member cooperatives as of February 2012

Classification			No of Cooperative
Regional Cooperative			968
Commodity Cooperative	Fruits		25
	Vegetables		17
	Horticulture		3
Regional Livestock			118
Livestock Commodity Cooperative	Dairy		13
		Swine	7
		Poultry	2
		Apiculture	1
		Rabbit & Deer	1
Ginseng Cooperative			12
Total			1,167

Operational restructuring

On 2 March 2012, the NACF restructured its operations, establishing financial

and marketing holding companies through the revised Agricultural Cooperative Law and a resolution of the <u>board of directors</u> on 2 February 2012. The new NACF performs as the center of the member cooperatives, governing the Extension and Support Unit, the Agricultural and Supply Business Unit, the Livestock Marketing and Supply Unit and the Cooperative Banking Unit.

Extension and support unit

The NACF supports the operations and management activities of member cooperatives by providing education and training for their members and working to promote the rights of farmers. It also provides <u>investments</u> to develop and promote new agricultural technologies and products.

Marketing and Supply units

The NACF provides marketing support for the production, <u>distribution</u>, processing, and consumption of agricultural and livestock products, focusing particularly on increasing the income of farming households by expanding sales channels and reducing farming costs. This enables farmers to concentrate their efforts on farming.

Cooperative Banking unit

The banking unit unit serves as an intermediary and facilitator, providing loan and deposit services for member cooperatives and engaging in other incidental businesses. As of 2011, the total deposit is KRW 209 trillion and the total loan volume is KRW 146 trillion.

Subsidiaries and Affiliated organizations

Financial holding company

The objective of the financial holding company and its subsidiaries is to secure the funds and revenues necessary for the intrinsic activities of the NACF, and to provide differentiated banking services to its customers. It offers diverse financial services such as <u>deposits</u>, <u>loans</u> credit cards, insurance, <u>foreign exchange</u>, and securities.

- NH Nonghyup Bank Co., Ltd
- Nonghyup Life Insurance Co., Ltd
- Nonghyup Property & Casualty Insurance Co., Ltd
- NH-CA Asset Management Co., Ltd
- NH Nonghyup Investment & Securities Co., Ltd.
- NH Nonghyup Investment & Futures Co., Ltd.
- NH Capital Co., Ltd.

Marketing holding company

 The objective of the marketing holding company and its subsidiaries is to vitalize the marketing and supply of agricultural and livestock products through advanced expertise and efficient product distribution.

- Korea Agricultural Cooperative Marketing Inc
- Namhae Chemical Corporation
- Young Il Chemical Co., Ltd
- Nonghyup Hansamin, Ltd.
- Nonghyup Logistics Service, Inc.
- Korea Agricultural Cooperative Trading Co., Ltd.
- Agricultural Cooperative Pusan Kyongnam Marketing, Inc.
- Agricultural Cooperative Chungbuk Marketing Co., Ltd.
- Daejeon Agricultural Products Marketing Center Co., Ltd.
- Nonghyup-Agro, Inc.
- Samhyup Nongsan Co., Ltd.
- Nonghyup Feed, Inc.
- Nonghyup Moguchon, Inc.

5. Rural Development Administration
http://www.rda.go.kr , rda@rda.go.kr

1).Overview

The Rural Development Administration (RDA) is the central government organization responsible for extensive agricultural research and services in Korea.

In the past, RDA helped Korea to achieve self-sufficiency in rice and other staple food through dissemination and promotion of high-yielding cultivars and improved cropping technologies, and made a remarkable progress in fresh vegetable production by introducing year-round cropping systems in greenhouses.

Furthermore, RDA contributed greatly to the improvement of the rural environment and nurturing new farmers.

The era of globalization is blooming in the agricultural sector as well, and Korean agriculture is struggling to cope with the new international trade environment and challenges.
RDA's efforts are directed towards highly competitive agriculture and efficient rural development. It endeavors to support farmers to produce agricultural commodities with better quality; advancing low-input, labor-saving and environment-friendly cropping technologies; promoting modern and automated production facilities; and nurturing future farmers

2). Brief History

Feb. 2004 Rank adjustment for strengthening policy and planning and reinforcement of researcher in ginseng area
Jan. 2004 Integrated National Honam Agricultural Experiment Station and National Yeongnam Agricultural Experiment Station into National Crop Experiment Station and reconstituted as National Institute of Crop Science (NICS)
Mar. 2002 Established the National Institute of Agricultural Bio-technology integrated the National Rural Living Science Institute into National Institute of Agricultural Science and Technology
Aug. 2000 Transferred the National Seed Management Office to MAF
Aug. 1998 Integrated the National Sericulture and Entomology Research Institute with the National Institute of Agricultural Science and Technology
Feb. 1998 Transferred the National Veterinary Research Institute to MAF
Feb. 1996 Established the Korea National Agricultural College under RDA
Dec. 1994 Reconstituted to incorporate the following offices previously under the Ministry of Agriculture and Forestry (MAF) : National Livestock Germplasm Office, National Agricultural Material Inspection Office, National Sericulture Office, National Seed Production and Distribution Office
Apr. 1962 Reorganized as the Rural Development Administration (RDA)
May 1957 Renamed as the Institute of Agriculture
Dec. 1947 Reconstituted as the Institute of Agricultural Improvement
Apr. 1906 Founded as the Agricultural Demonstration Station

3). Organization

- Administrator
- Planning and Management Officer
- Research Management Bureau
- Farm Management and Information Officer

- Extension Bureau
- National Institute of Agricultural Science and Technology
- National Institute of Crop Science
- National Institute of Agricultural Biotechnology
- National Institute of Agricultural Engineering
- Honam Agricultural Research Institute. NICS
- Yeongnam Agricultural Research Institute, NICS
- National Horticultural Research Institute
- National Institute of Highland Agriculture
- Korea National Agricultural College
- National Institute of Subtropical Agriculture
- National Livestock Research Institute

4). Fields of Activity

- Research and Development of agricultural technologies
- Dissemination of agricultural technologies and extension services
- Quality control of fertilizers, pesticides and agro machineries
- Guidance and training for rural development and home improvement
- Climate and soil research
- Crop Research
- Sustainable agriculture Research
- Biotechnology Research
- Bio-resource Research
- Horticultural research
- Livestock and veterinary research
- Rural living science research

III. Beginning and Evolution of Saemaul Undong

1.Economic Status before Saemaul Undong

Generally speaking, social movement takes place without any well-defined format or theoretical framework. Hence, human being's activities take shape through pattern of "learning by doing". Without exemption, this guiding principle is applicable to the Saemaul Undong. Such a case is clearly shown in several rural development movements i.e. Patriot Yun's Rural Rehabilitation Movement campaigned against illiteracy in rural villages under Japanese rule.

Any and all social movements, reflect the society's cultural traits interim of historical and spiritual stance. In this context, the Saemaul Undong is genuinely unique to Korea. Saemaul literally means a new village, the Saemaul Undong represents a social movement to improve the quality of life through cooperative efforts. The sweat and toil of a great number of participants in the Saemaul Undong has enabled Korea's rural villages to attain its present state. Theories and strategies developed as the movement progressed and the accumulated outcome of the movement led to the reduction of the income gap between rural and urban areas. Therefore, in the 1980s, there is the need of Saemaul Undong to be systematically realigned for further promotion and sophistication.

In the incipient stage of economic development, what is important is the creation of the wealthier nation and not the distribution of the accumulated wealth. Only after the establishment of wealth can we consider the distribution of it. This is exemplified by the change in the Saemaul Undong from "the movement for well-being" in the 1970s to "the movement for all to be well-off" in the 1980s. In principle, any and all great achievements can be attained, first by means of the creation of wealth and then by striving to achieve equitable distribution of the accumulated wealth.

It seems that the people's zeal and positive attitudes were equally important in bringing about the success of the Saemaul Undong in the 1970s. Therefore, credit must go to all participants, Saemaul leaders and field workers alike, for the success of the movement.On the strength of the success of the Saemaul Undong over the last decades, we must now share the experience of Saemaul Undong not only for rural areas but in urban communities of developing countries as well. In order to meet this goal, we need the voluntary participation of all the beginner's people who can take part in the continued march towards the further development of this country. In doing so, a positive contribution in minimizing the gap between urban and rural sectors could be made in terms of the state welfare as well as the accumulation of wealth.

1). Rural Korea in the 1950s and 1960s.

In the early 1960s, Korea's industrial development benefited urban areas more
than the rural populace. Due to the nature of agriculture and geographical
situation of rural communities, farmers are unable to affiliate with urban
institutions, and thus they failed to partake in the ensuing benefits.The
differences in the standard of living between the rural and urban populace are
primarily not a result of any genuine difference in their cultural values or
hereditary abilities, but rather a consequence of small arable land resources
relative to the population in rural Korea. Yet, until the late 1960s, the Korean
government did little to modernize the rural situation.Due to ever-increasing
budgetary requirements for the reconstruction of the war-devastated
economy and national security outlay, funds available for government aid
were extremely limited. The low price policy for farm products was further
reinforced by the easy availability of American grains on concessionaire
terms under the PL 480 Program, concluded between Korea and the United
States in 1955. Although the importation of relief grains has contributed a
great deal to ensuring a stable food grain supply and general economic
stability, it obviously has not stimulated policy makers to increase the
domestic production of food grains by adopting a positive price policy. The
government purchased price for rice remained lower than the estimated cost
of production in almost every year until the late 1960s.
By the late 1960s, a fundamental change in the situation forced the
government to reorient the agricultural policy. While the rural people became
increasingly conscious of the widening gap in the standard of living between
the urban and rural populace, thegovernment began to perceive evidence of a
declining political support in rural areas in sharp contrast to the situation
noted in previous elections. The decline in the political popularity impelled
the government to shift mist priority to rural development. From 1969, the
purchasing prices of rice and barley steadily increased the government
improved the terms of trade in favor of agricultural producers.

To understand the Saemaul Undong, it is needed to review the general
economic background which necessitated the movement in the early 1970s,
and then the main features of the movement with reference its basic ideology
and contents could be clear. The organizational arrangements and
implementation process should also be introduced along with the strategic
operational rules adopted by the government. Finally, attempts should also be
made to understand criticisms and lessons based on past experiences as well
as some alternatives for institutional reform for rural development domestic
and abroad in the future.

2).Economic Development

Korea was a typical agrarian country until the early 1960s, with almost half of its GNP produced by agriculture and the majority of its population depended on farming. The industrialization efforts and export drive undertaken in the early 1960's have led to rapid economic growth and have transformed the agrarian character of the economy. The relative share of the primary sector in gross domestic product declined from about 37% in 1960 to 14% in 1982 and the proportion of farm population declined from 58% to less than 25%. There has also been a substantial shift in the composition of industrial output towards more sophisticated manufactured products.During these decades of hectic industrial development, industry and new employment were heavily concentrated in the urban areas. Transportation, and many economic and administrative institutions have all grown up to accelerate industrialization and business. The corporate business organization, banking system, credit facilities, and trade organizations are all urban institutions eminently suited to industrial and business needs. Industrial development and urbanization have had the further effect of benefiting urban citizens more than rural peoples. As a result, modernized facilities were hopelessly inapplicable to the need of farmers, since the nature of the agricultural process has prevented farmers from taking advantage of these urban institutions and partaking in their benefits. The only way to take chances of good jobs, better income and better education was to move from rural areas to urban areas.These differences in quality of living are not primarily the results of any original differences in the cultural values or hereditary abilities of the people themselves, but are basically consequences of poor resource endowment, especially limited land resources relative to population in rural Korea, and also the result of the way in which economic policy was executed in the past. Yet until the late 1960s the government did not or rather could not do much to change the rural situation. In more concrete terms, there are two discernable factors which are responsible for persistent rural poverty.

The 1st Factor

The marginality of land holding inherent to Korean agriculture and the negative farm price policy throughout the 1950s and 1960s.
The general historical pattern of agricultural development in Europe maybe described as a continuous process of farming scale expansion accompanied by technological progress. That is, progress in agricultural technology enlarges disparities in products capabilities among individual farmers within the same rural area. This leads to a disintegration of those classes of farmers with low productive capabilities, enabling the more successful farmers to remain on farms and expand the scale of economies. This, in turn, facilitates

the introduction of advanced technology centered around farm mechanization. Such a chain of cause and effect has been consistently evolving. In contrast, Korea's agriculture has long been characterized by the rigidity in its small holder structure form under the pressure of surplus population. This rigidity in size of farming restricts the adoption of new technology. Technical stagnation in turn impedes the improvement of agricultural productivity. This vicious cycle has constantly repeated itself.

Most of all problems confronting Korean agriculture stems from its small holder nature. Whereas, the exodus of rural labor can be considered conductive to the growth of labor productivity through an adoption of new technology such as farm machinery,and the structural marginality of land holdings is undoubtedly impeding such progress.Since the early 1960s, government has been striving to improve the agrarian structure, but little has been achieved in terms of enlarging the scale of land holding due to the limited land resources. Many people began to advocate an easing or even a repeal of the three hectare ceiling on individual ownership of farmland. The idea is to expedite concentration of land holdings in the hands of a smaller number of farmers by increasing the transferability of land titles.

Thus far the trend has been that the rate of decrease in number of farm-households has been much lower than that of farm population. As a result, the average size of farm land per household has remained almost static at about 1 ha. for the past two decades as shown in Tables 9 and 10.

Table9. Cultivated Acreage, Rural Pop, No of Farm Households, and Average Farm Size, 1965-80

Year	TotalCultivatedAcreage (1,000 ha)	TotalRural Population (1,000)	Average Size of Holdings(ha)	AverageSizeof FarmFamily (persons)
1965	2,275	15,812	0.91	6.3
1970	2,295	14,432	0.93	5.8
1975	2,240	13,244	0.94	5.6
1980	2,196	10,831	1.02	5.1

It should be noted that those farmers who cultivate 1 ha. or less constitute more than one third of the total number of farm households.

Table10. Distribution of Farm Households by Size of Holding, 1965-80

Year	Total	0.5 ha. or less	0.5- 1.0 ha.	1.0- 1.5 ha.	1.5- 2.0 ha.	2.0- 3.0 ha.	3.0- or more
1965	100.0	35.0	31.6	16.5	9.3	5.6	1.2
1970	100.0	31.6	34.3	18.5	8.0	5.1	1.5

| 1975 | 100.0 | 30.3 | 36.2 | 18.9 | 8.2 | 4.8 | 1.6 |
| 1980 | 100.0 | 28.8 | 35.0 | 20.6 | 9.0 | 5.1 | 1.5 |

This small holding of farmland, aside from various policy measures, is a major constraint on expanding agricultural labor productivity and farm income.

The 2nd Factor

The persistent negative farm price policy, particularly for major grains.During the 1950s the government's main efforts were directed toward the rehabilitation of the war wrecked economy as well as the alleviation of postwar inflation. Policy makers were particularly sensitive to the effects of grain prices on the urban wage earners' costs of living and on inflation. Efforts were centered on depressing prices of grain at low levels. Government investment and loans to agriculture were severely limited due to the increasing budgetary requirement for rehabilitation work and defense purposes. About all the budget was capable of financing in the agricultural sector were maintenance for existing irrigation facilities and importation of fertilizer.

The low farm price policy was further reinforced by the easy availability of American grain on concessionary terms under the Public Law 480 program, concluded in 1955. Although the importation of aid has contributed significantly to a stable food supply and general economic stability, it has obviously caused a disincentive for policy makers to increase domestic production of food grain by means of a positive price policy. The government purchase prices for rice remained lower than the estimated costs of production in almost every year until 1960. The government grain was in effect requisitioned compulsorily from famers through local administrative channels. Table 11 gives the total estimated loss on the part of famers due to low of rice between 1952 and 1960, and indicates how the low grain price policy contributed in a major way to rural poverty.

Table 11. Farmers' Financial Losses from Sales to government

Crop Year	Quantity of Sales (100MT)	Government Price (won/80kg)	Cost of Production (won/80kg)	Loss (won/80kg)	Total Loss (10^{6}won)
1952	268	200.62	329.09	128.47	430
1953	517	200.62	330.94	130.32	642
1954	347	308.33	330.94	22.61	98
1955	389	390.56	838.14	447.58	2,176
1956	286	1,059.00	1,134.00	75.00	268
1957	175	1,059.00	1.394.00	335.00	733
1958	168	1,059.00	1,297.00	238.00	500
1959	198	1,059.00	1,300.00	241.00	594

| 1960 | 141 | 1,059.00 | 1,313.00 | 254.00 | 448 |

Source: Ministry of Agriculture and Fisheries, <u>AgriculturalStatisticsYearbook</u>

Entering the 1960s the economy was gradually rehabilitated from its war-damaged state, and the major emphasis of economic policy was shifted from rehabilitation and stability to expansion. The basic goal of the policy (as envisaged in the first and second five-year economic plans) was to build a foundation on which to attain self-sustaining economic goal. The terms "equitable income distribution between rural and urban household" and "increased domestic food production have appeared in almost every policy document as the determined objectives of agricultural policy. Yet they had to remain only as paper slogans. Then farm price support program was again put off. Because general price stabilization was listed as a top priority, the policy emphasis continued to be placed on maintaining prices of farm products as low as possible in investment policies, the industrial sector received high priority in sharing financial resources. The high weight of grain both the wholesale and consumer price indices made the maintenance of low grain prices a key anti-inflationary instrument.There was another change of more fundamental nature by the late 1960s, which almost impelled the regime to reorient the policy toward agriculture. Rural people became increasingly conscious of the widening standard of living gap between city and country.Historically, beginning with the establishment of the government in 1948, rural voters tended to support passively whichever regime happened to be in power, despite its pursuit of urban-biased economic policies. But the situation has changed.The late government began to perceive evidence of a decline in rural political support, in contrast to the situation in previous elections.It is this consciousness of a decline in political that spurred the regime to shift its emphasis toward rural development. Starting with the 1969 crops. The price at which the government purchased rice and barley were steadily increased with a view to improving the terms of trade in favor of farm producers. The initiation of higher purchase prices for major grains clearly reflected a dramatic change in agricultural price and was part of the government effort to stimulate domestic production of food grain and upgrade farm incomes. Another major shift in policy was the initiation of massive scale investment in the rural development sphere.

2. Beginning of Saemaul Undong

1).Beginning of Saemaul Project

A drastic change had occurred in government policy towards rural development of Korea by the early 1970's. The change was the Saemaul Undong started in the winter of 1971/72. From the beginning, the Saemaul

Undong was initiated by the government for rural development.With government support, huge scale investment projects were carried out for infrastructure and strengthening rural people's attitudes through a series of spiritual enlightenment campaigns and adult education. During the process of the Saemaul Undong, rural people also mobilized as much as they could in terms of resources and effort. As a result, both of rural infrastructure and living environment had been eye popping improved. The Saemaul Undong contributed greatly to transform every corner of rural Korea during the 1970s.After ten years of experience, the Saemaul Undong is being subjected to various criticisms because of its top-down authoritarian approaches. The authoritarian administration rather hindered rural villagers' voluntary participation and even caused to mal-location of resources during the process of implementation.

It is generally agreed that the starting point of the Saemaul Undong in Korea is related to a disposal of surplus cement. In 1971 cement production far exceeded demand, causing an excessive inventory in the country. After a series of inter-ministerial meetings, a decision was made to use the surplus cement for productive purposes in rural areas.

The government provided 335 bags of cement, free of charge, equally to each of a total 33,267 villages during the winter season of 1970/71. The recipient villagers were instructed to use the cement only for the purpose of meeting villagers ' common needs based upon village consensus. At the local level, about 20 potential projects on average were recommended by the local administrations:

- Improvement of farm roads,
- Establishment of a sanitary water supply system,
- Sewage improvements,
- River dike repairs,
- Construction of common wells,
- Public laundry places, and so forth

The program was widely welcomed by villagers, who found good uses for the cement, and the results greatly exceeded the expectations of the government officials. Encouraged by the performance of the rural people, the government selected 16,600 villages, which had responded actively and had successfully carried out their projects. In 1972 the government supplied an additional 500 bags of cement together with one ton of steel rods to each of these selected villages.

Further encouraged by this experimentation, the Ministry of Home Affairs conducted a nationwide village survey, and classified all the villages in the country into three categories on the basis of degree of performance and level of development:

(1) Basic (underdeveloped)village,
(2) Self-help(developing) village,
(3) Self-reliant (developed) village.

Based upon this classification, the government adopted different approaches for different classes of village. Greater assistance was given to higher level villages. This differential approach was intended to create a sense of competition among villages and to stimulate those villages in the lower classes to make more efforts toward advantages to a higher villages classes. Each village was required to accomplish a minimum performance prior to advancement in the classification scheme.
Having observed this early experience, the late government authorities began to take a keen interest and ordered the program intensified and extending. They also emphasized the importance of identifying motivated village leaders as well as the need for education and training

2).Process and Philosophy of Saemaul Undong

The Saemaul Undong has developed through the following stages:
- The first stage (1971-1973): Initiation of the Saemaul Undong;
- The second stage (1974-1976): Period of extensive development of the Saemaul Undong;
- The third stage (1977~1980): Completion of self-reliant posture:
- The fourth stage (1980 ~ 1987): Period of many-fold of Saemaul Undong.
- The fifth stage (1988 ~ 1999): Period of slump and stagnation of Saemaul Undong.
- The sixth stage(2000 ~ to date): Period of Global Sharing of Korean Experience

As mentioned earlier, Rural Saemaul Undong was launched in 1971 in the midst of the unbalanced socio-economic development between urban and rural areas. From its inception, the movement was implemented without any defined theoretical framework. In the process of its revolution, higher goals, spirit and strategies for the drive were implemented and thus, the movement has moved on as implemented on the influence all existing sectors of Korean society.

As known well, the Saemaul Undong played a pivotal role in the socioeconomic development of Korea.

<u>Basic Ideology and Contents</u>

According to one official definition of the Ministry of Home Affairs, "Saemaul Undong (movement) is a new community movement in which people cooperate together in order to construct better and richer villages, and as a consequence, a richer and stronger nation." In order words , the Saemaul Undong is a Korean model of the regional community development with the ultimate goal of creating an advanced and strong nation through constructing a dynamic and affluent society .In order to achieve the above stated ultimate goal, three specific objectives are further enunciated from a strategic viewpoint;

(1) Spiritual reform,
(2) Social renovation,
(3) Economic development.

Spiritual reform aims at enhancing rural villagers' willingness and confidence in self-reliance. It aims at promoting the spirit of self-help, diligence, and mutual cooperation, which are the moral foundation for the introduction of rural innovation to come. The spirit of self-help emphasizes the importance of identifying oneself in a correct perspective and solving one's own problems with one's own efforts, and thereby encourages rural people to change deeprooted fatalistic attitudes. Korean farmers traditionally adhered to the notion that poverty was their fate; something they could not manage for themselves.

The core of the spirit of diligence is a sound work ethic without which no one or no country can pursue a better and more affluent life. The spirit of diligence is fostered through villagers' voluntary and active participation in the activities of common interest. Diligence is also bound to be accompanied by the spirit of austerity and saving. The spirit of diligence and thrift is of vital importance for the people in underdeveloped countries which have limited natural resources, capital, and technology.

The spirit of cooperation emphasizes the importance of cooperative and group in achieving common goals which are beyond the capacity of individuals. This spirit of cooperation helps to change people's attitudes toward greater solidarity in their daily activities as well as toward national integrity. The spirit of cooperation is particularly important for a country like Korea where the rapid industrialization tend to isolate people from each other and create selfish, egocentric individualism.

Historically, a majority of Korean people had been long subjected to various forms of exploitation by the ruling classes of successive dynasties, and more recently had suffered from painful squeezes during the Japanese colonial period. The political and socio-economic system were such that voluntary participation in self-improving, production activities was largely discouraged. Moreover, the extended family system combined with an authoritarian power structure severely restricted development of individualism and decision-making abilities. People tended to be dependent upon outside decisions and help. They lacked confidence in themselves and were not able even to realize their own potential or what they could achieve for the betterment of their own lives.Under these circumstances, spiritual enlightenment was regarded as indispensable in the Saemaul Undong as a means of changing the value systems and attitudes toward a new way of life. At this moment, various training and educational programs were designed and extensively implemented, in addition to the physical aspects of the movement.

Social Renovation.

Social renovation aspects of the Saemaul Undonginclude those programs which aim at improving the environment in whichvillagers' lives. Since rural people are increasingly conscious of differences in environment between urban and rural living, narrowing the urban-rural gap in the level of living standards received top priority in the movement. The social development programs are classified into three sub-categories:

(1) Environment improvement;
(2) Housing improvement; and
(3) Public utilityexpansion.

Each program is further divided into individual projects. Environmentprograms include the establishment of sanitary water supply systems, improved sewage systems, public bathhouses, village conference halls, publicwells, village laundry yards, and so on. Housing improvement projects include roof improvement, house repairs, and village restructuring. Public utility expansion programs comprise two major individual projects: expansion of rural electrification and communication networks, especially the installation of public telephones in villages.

Economic Development

The economic development program comprisestwo major categories;

(1) Build-up production infrastructure,
(2) An income augmentation program.

Included in the production infrastructureprogram are farm road expansion and small-scale irrigation projects such asconstruction of wells, irrigation ponds, and irrigation and drainage roads so that tractors, trucks, and other farm machinery can pass, as well as to connect village roads to fields and main roads. This project made a significant contribution to facilitating farm mechanization and transportation services even in remote areas.Small-scale irrigation projects brought forth another important infrastructure improvement, contributing to fostering agricultural productivity. A considerable portion of the existing irrigation and drainage system was obsolete or nearing obsolescence due to lack of repair work over many years. Recovering the original capacity of these facilities was urgently needed.All these infrastructure projects were in the nature of social overhead capital in villages. And as most of the projects were of the labor-intensive type, they could be carried out with indigenous technology which was available locally. Outside assistance was obtained for only those works which required more or less high-level know-how. Since these works were undertaken during the off-season, when labor mobilization was relatively easy, the rate of return on capital was expected to be high.Included in the income augmentation program are livestock raising, introduction of cash crops, development of specialized production areas, and group farming, and the establishment of Saemaul factories to increase off-farm income sources. The area specialization protect consists of four major categories; general cropsand vegetables, livestock, and cash crops production areas. This integrated package program was initiated. The package programs integrate various projects of infrastructure buildups,production, and marketing facilities, farm mechanization, and so forth.In addition to these income augmentation projects, the government providedvarious kinds of support-financial and technical-for constructing Saemaulfactories in order to increase employment opportunities during the off-season

3.Major Development of the Movement

In the initial stage of the movement, the main emphasis was placed uponthose Projects of improving the living environment, such as piped water supplysystems, sewage improvements, public wells, and so forth. But passing throughthis initial stage of implementation, an important lesson has emerged In regardto selection of type of project. The lesson was that projects should be selectedso as to contribute immediately to upgrading villagers' income position.Although the environmental improvements provide direct benefits in dailyliving and contribute to enhancing hope for life in the future, were improvement in surroundings without accompanying income growth may limply inflate people's desires. The tangible results as perceived by villagers are of practical significance in promoting adaptability to changing rural conditionsand technological progress.Thus, from the mid-1970s the emphasis shifted from environment-oriented

Projects to income-generating ones. The government set a target for increasingaverage farm income to 1.4 million won (approximately U. S. $3,500) by 1981,the target year concluding the fourth five-year economic plan. In order toachieve this goal. A number of income augmentation projects were introducedand government support programs were provided extensively for the projectsin the form of subsidy and credit.Major categories of income augmentation programs were;

(1) Regionalspecialization of crops;
(2) Livestock raising;
(3) Group farming and marketing, effectively.

Especially in the field of crop production, all the villages were encouragcd to organize 'Saemaul production units" for group farming, withevery farmer belonging to at least one unit. Rural women were also encouragedto organize "Saemaul women's clubs" and the existing 4-H Clubs were renamed "Saemaul Youth Clubs," all to participate more actively in the Saemaulmovement. A ".Saemaul Credit Union" was also organized in each villageunder government support to promote the spirit of thrift and saving, and acampaign was launched to induce every farmer to maintain a savings accountin the union.

Extensive Participation and Investment

It has been widely advocated that the extensive participation of individualsand groups is of prime importance for any community development movement.Participation is the major element of community development which distinguishes it from other forms of social and economic policy. The Saemaul movement of Korea is probably unprecedented in terms of scope of participation. Having started from rural village-centered environmental Improvementprojects, the movement has rapidly expanded both in scope of participation and range of program activities. It has extended to "Factory Saemaul," "Urban Saemaul," and further to "School Saemaul." One can see the Saemaul flag flying along with the national flag and Saemaul slogan painted at the top of almost every public building throughoutthe country. At least once a day there is a television program displaying asuccess story of the Saemaul movement, accompanied by the Saemaul song.As suggested by cynics, everyone is involved in doing everything under thename of Saemaul. This fact alone is sufficient to explain how wide participation in the movement has been, and how enthusiastically it was launched on a nationwide basis. In order to grasp the picture more clearly, a numericalpresentation seems to be in orderan official record compiled by the Ministry of Home Affairs indicates thatmore than 36,000 villages have participated in the Saemaul movement everyyear since 1972. This means that almost every village in Korea-

eitherlargeor small in scale-has been engaged in the movement. The Participation in ruralareas alone has increased from 32 million workdays in 1972 to 117 millionworkdays in 1975 and further to 273 million workdays in 1982. Calculatedn per village terms, the participation was 923 workdays in 1972, increasingto 3,160 workdays in 1975, and again to 7,380 workdays in 1982-an almosteightfold increase over a ten-year period. Assuming 60 farm households pervillage, this implies that each household was devoting on average about 123workdays (or four months' time) to Saemaul activities in 1982.The rapid expansion in activities can also be grasped by the increasingnumber of individual projects undertaken over the safe 2,667,000 in 1979-8.3 times as many as in 1972. Since then, the number of projects has graduallydeclined and a total of 1,310,000 projects was implemented in 1981 (seeTable 10).

Table 10. Scope of Participation in the Saemaul Undong, 1972-81

Year	Number of Villages	Number of Villagers (1,000)	Number of Projects (1,000)	Number of Projects per Village	Investment Per project (1,000won)
1972	34,665	32,000	320	14	98
1973	34,665	69,280	1,093	32	90
1974	34,665	106,852	1,099	32	121
1975	36,574	116,880	1,598	44	185
1976	36,574	117,528	887	24	364
1977	36,574	137,198	2,463	67	189
1978	36,257	270,928	2,667	74	237
1979	36,271	242,078	2,788	49	424
1980	36,938	227,856	1,836	51	510
1981	36,792	257,472	1,310	35	537

Source: Ministry of home Affairs, The Saemaul Undong from Its beginning Until Today, issues 1972-81.

The scope of participation can be further demonstrated in terms of villager'scontributions including each, labor, land, and materials. In 1972 a total 31.6 billion won was invested in the Saemaul projects, of which rural peoplecontributed 27.3 billion won or 86.6%, while the government financialassistance amounted to only 36 billion won or 11.3%.But as the movement has proceeded, the relative shares between the twosources have become reversed, although the absolute amount of investmenthas increased.

The proportion of people's contributions declined to 57.3% in 1975 and dropped further to 34.4% in 1982. Conversely,the government provision increased to 114 billion won or 42.1% in 1971 and again increased to 419 billion won or 42.3% in 1982, the rest beingdonated by various private organizations. Thus the major components of funding sources has shifted from villagers to government financial assistancein report years. This is because an increasing number of development activities has been added to the Saemaul category under government sponsorship.Amount of investment per project also rapidly increased, forom318,000 won in 1972 to 702,000 won in 1981(see Table11).

Table 11 Investment in Saemaul Projects, 1972-81:Government vs. Villagers

Year	Total Investment		Government Support		Villagers' Contribution[a]		Others[b]	
	Amount (10^9 won)	Share (%)	Amount (10^9 won)	Share (%)5	Amount (10^9 won)	Share (%)	Amount (10^9 won)	Share (%)
1972	31.6	100.0	3.6	11.3	27.3	86.6	0.7	2.1
1973	96.1	100.0	17.1	17.0	76.9	80.0	2.1	2.2
1974	132.8	100.0	30.8	23.1	98.7	74.4	3.3	2.5
1975	295.9	100.0	124.5	42.1	169.6	57.3	1.8	0.6
1976	322.7	100.0	88.1	27.3	227.4	70.5	7.2	2.2
1977	466.5	100.0	138.1	29.6	325.0	69.7	3.4	0.7
1978	634.2	100.0	145.7	23.0	487.8	76.9	0.7	0.1
1979	758.2	100.0	425.2	56.1	328.2	43.3	4.0	0.6
1980	936.0	100.0	na	Na	na	na	Na	na
1981	702.9	100.0	415.6	59.2	282.6	40.2	4.7	0.6

Source: Ministry of Home Affairs, The Saemaul Undong: From Its Beginning until Today, issues1972-81
Notes: na signifies not available,
a Includes loans and credit
b Donations from non-government organizations.

Table 12 presents a breakdown of villagers` contributions by category. Contributions in the form of labor accounted for 77.2% in 1972 but had declined to only 25.2% by 1982. As a process of cash substitution tookplace, the major part of villagers` contributions shifted from labor to cash.

Table 12 Villagers' Contribution by Item, 1972-82

Year	Contribution		Cash		Labor[a]		Materials		Land[b]	
	Amount (10^9 won)	Share (%)	Amount(10^9 won)	Share (%)	Amount (10^9 won)	Share (%)	Amount (10^9 won)	Share (%)	Amount(10^9 won)	Share (%)
1972	27.3	100.0	na	Na	21.1	77.2	5.2	19.2	1.0	3.6
1973	76.9	100.0	na	Na	na	na	na	Na	Na	Na

1974	98.7	100.0	32.6		33.1	54.1	54.8	10.1	10.2	1.9	1.9
1975	169.6	100.0	94.3		55.6	63.9	37.6	8.6	5.1	2.8	1.6
1976	227.4	100.0	133.8		58.8	78.2	34.4	12.6	5.5	2.9	1.3
1977	325.0	100.0	188.4		58.0	96.3	29.6	33.7	10.4	6.5	2.0
1978	487.8	100.0	300.0		62.7	102.4	21.0	32.3	3.8	36.6	7.5
1979	328.2	100.0	191.7		58.4	118.5	36.1	15.4	4.7	2.6	0.3
1980	Na	na	na		Na	na	na	na	Na	Na	Na
1981	282.6	100.0	173.8		61.5	85.1	30.1	18.7	6.6	5.2	1.0
1982	298.1	100.0	200.3		67.2	75.1	25.2	20.6	6.9	2.1	0.7

Source: Ministry of Home Affairs, The Saemaul Undong from Its Beginning until Today, issues1972-81.
Notes: na signifies not available
a Evaluated at current wages.
b Evaluated at current prices.

4. Extensive Saemaul Education

Through the process of early experimentation in implementing various projects for the improvement lessen. That is, the existence of leadership is a prerequisite for self-reliant and self-sustaining community development. This is because efficient village leaders play the most crucial role in inducing villagers' participation in the Saemaul Undong.

Various types of leadership training institutions were established, beginning in late 1972. The Saemaul Training institute was established as the main training institute at the central level. Successively fourteen other central level and ten provincial level training institutions were formed under government sponsorship. And also various types of informal training programs were provided at the country and village level. Potential Saemaul loaders were identified and elected from among villagers and offered a special training program that aimed at equipping them with effective leadership in playing roles as agents of change in rural areas. As the movement progressed, village women loaders, youth loaders, and local officials were included in the training program from 1973.

Starting from 1974 the social elite class and government officials were also included. In 1975 the training program was further intensified in quality and expanded in scope or participation, to include all classes of social leaders such as parliamentarians, religious leaders, university professors, journalists, managers of business corporations, and so forth. In training these non-farmer elites, the main emphasis was placed uponencouraging them to participate positively as well as to give full support to the basic ideology and strategy of the Saemaul Uudong. They were to receive the training together with village leaders under the same conditions, regardless of their social status, with a view to bringing them closer to rural situations and fostering the spirit of solidarity. The training not only provided class lectures but also emphasized self-learning through case studies, group discussions, andfield tours based on the "learning·by-doing" principle.

IV. GOs, NGOs and Strategies

1.Leader's Philosophy and Strategies

Korean Five-Years PlanBoth of the First Five -Year Plan (62-66) and the Second plan (67-71) emphasized industrialization over agriculture and rural development. Results exceeded expectations. The average rate of economic growth between 1962-73 was 9.6 %, one of the highest in the world. The gross national product rose to 12.4 billion dollars in 1973, 5.9 times of the 2.1 billion dollars GNP of 1961 before economic plans started in Korea. Meanwhile, the per capital GNP increased from 83 dollars in 1961 to more than 500 dollars in 1975.Despite this remarkable economic growth, the government of Korea was not free from its critics. A great disparity between rural and urban areas still exists. A large percentage of rural families owned less than a half hectare of land, less than the minimum considered necessary to support a family. The average family holding is only about 1hectare. This large percentage of rural families owning less than sufficient land for self-support, plus the fact that they were not satisfactorily employed, meant that agriculture remained a retarded industry incapable of overcoming severe income in equality with the urban areas and of producing a self-sufficient food supply. Moreover, rural emigrants to urban areas for new jobs had increased to such an extent that the proportion of rural population dropped by almost 10percent, from56.5 in 1961 to 45.9 in 1970, thus creating a rural labor shortage.
Accordingly, the Third Five-Year Plan (72-77) emphasized the followings;

- development of agriculture,
- self-sufficiency in food production,
- increase the farmers' income, and
- improvement of rural living conditions.

As well known in April 1970, at a meeting of the provincial governors and mayors. President Park Chung Hee proposed a new village movement that would greatly improve the environment in rural areas. He told the gathering that "self-helping" villages, in his view, could overcome rural poverty problems, while those depending on others could not. Implementation of this program was initiated during the period of October, 1970.

The government's evaluation of this pilot project, in July 1971, disclosed that its expenditure of approximately $11,000,000 for the cement resulted in village improvements valued at $32,600,000 results worth nearly three times the government's investment. But the evaluation also revealed that some villages failed to make self-help improvements with the cement provided, while others were quite successful. After analyzing the causes of these disparities, the Ministry of Home Affairs concluded that the quality of village leadership was the key factor determining success or failure.

Development Goals and Strategies

According to scholars such as Dudley Sears, Gary S. Fields, M.J. Ulmer, and L.A. Hoffman, the development of a society means reduction of poverty, unemployment and inequality. Hence, human development is an important goal in the development of a society. Taking into consideration the important role of the economy as a tool for living, maximization of individual welfare extends to maximizing society's well-being. From this point of view, the economic welfare referred to in this paper is summarized and defined as the increased in real income distribution and stable economic growth.

The goal of Saemaul Undong is the realization of a democratic welfare community through a people's attitude change. The change of attitude can be realized by putting into practice the concepts of the Saemaul Undong represented by diligence, self-help and cooperation.

.

There are many points to be considered in order to realize the goal of rural development such as:

- Rural policy and administrative support;
- Innovation of agricultural technologies including storage and processing;
- Promotion of cooperative farming and cooperatives;
- Improvement of marketing facilities and system;
- Farm machanization;
- Strengthening the positive attitude of farmers;
- Accumulation of rural community funds; and facilities;
- Enhancing grassroots' potential.and participation

Among others, it is essential to accumulate community funds for use in rural development. Since fund raising can make agriculture and community development moving. Doing so, the equitable development between rural and urban areas can be easily achieved. At this point, it is useful to perform an analysis of several cases of rural development. Then, it can clearly be understood to what extent the above factors were instrumental in enhancing rural development In this point of view, Korean cooperative heritages have very muchdedicated in the country's development.

Adult Education and Spiritual Change

President Park thereupon ordered his Ministry of Agriculture and Fisheries to devise a plan that would develop village leadership among villagers themselves. Having himself experienced rural poverty in his early years, the President stressed that rural development required attitudinal change of farmers toward the values of self-help, diligence, and cooperation, which could be formed through educational and environmental changes.

To ignite the "new village movement, "village leaders must be motivated to sacrifice themselves for others.The resulting plan proposed by the Ministry of Agriculture and Fisheries, accepted by the President and implemented, constitutes a completely indigenous program that does not reflect in its main features the experience or models of other Asian nations.On January 31, 1972, a main feature of the plan became reality with the opening of the Farmers Training Center, later known as the Saemaul Leaders Training Institute, to train village leaders. From its beginning in 1972 through 1975, the Institute has trained 17,000 persons, with an average of a one-week course for each trainee. Besides Saemaul leaders from the villages, the Institute has trained many government officials, including professors, students and journalists. These members of the urban and social elite engage in all Institute activities with the village leaders in the class rooms, in the dining hall, and on the playing field. Common uniforms and schedules tend to obscured rank and status distinctions. Doing so, the government could succeed to reduce rural-urban differences and class barriers.

The main purpose of the Institute was not to impart instruction in agricultural techniques. Rather, the principal objective was to change mental attitudes of Saemaul leaders by infusing the so-called Saemaul spirits among trainees.

The Institute's program represented the government's recognition of the importance of ideology for the motivation and mobilization, through village leaders. Consisting of much more than idealistic rhetoric, the program was a systematic attempt to institutionally produce altruistic leaders who would infuse among their villagers, the stated values of integrity, self-help, cooperation, scientific rationalism, and an optimistic view of life.

In the President Park's public statements; his New Year's message of January, 1976, he said:

"Thanks to the great effort made in the Saemaul spirit of diligence, self-help and cooperation, the conditions of rural life have been enormously improved…"

Environmental improvement, a main objective of the Saemaul Undong, was to create a healthy, rational and productive rural environment. Saemaul projects range from improvement of village roads, roofs, and walls to anti-erosion projects. These activities were funded in part by the central government. Acting on the knowledge gained from the 1971 pilot project, the government in 1972 gave 500 bags of cement and one ton of reinforcing steel to each of 16,600 villages deemed successful in 1971. Although none was distributed at that time to the unsuccessful villages, an additional 6,108 villages joined the 1972 program later in the year. The 1972 projects completed were valued at a high point of 8.8 times the investment cost compared to the 1971 results valued at 2.9 times the cost and 1973 results valued at 4.3 times. Reasons for variation of these government-preferred "efficiency" rates, and their method of computation to represent its version of 1971–1974 progress.

Strategies and Development Goals
In 1973, the government classified villages into three categories according to their stages of development: undeveloped (basic), developing (self-help), and developed (self-sufficient) villages. The grouping was made according to various criteria, the most explicit of which is the common funds each village had available for Saemaul projects:
- undeveloped: below $1,250;
- developing: over $1,250; and
- developed: over $2,500.
- Undeveloped villages, moreover, were considered to lack of organization and leadership as well as the resources required to carry out projects and, therefore, required educational and financial assistance from the government to initiate self-help projects. Accordingly, emphasis in undeveloped villages was placed on environmental improvement and provision of necessary infra-structure.
- The developing villages were considered to have acquired leadership and organizational ability to identify and carry out village projects, but lack the financial resources to implement them and also require government support. The developing villages, therefore, were primarily concerned with the expansion of infra-structure and income.
- The developed villages, on the other hand, were considered to be those that have carried out environmental improvement projects, significantly raised rural income, and achieved some degree of financial viability so that they could finance additional rural development projects from their own resources. Thus, the developed villages stressed the increase of income and the improvement of welfare.
The government's goal is for all villages to be "developed" by 1981. Program became national with the classification of all villages into three categories in 1973, the Saemaul Undong became a national movement. Emphasis was also shifted from projects to improve the environment, to projects for increasing income, including the collective cultivation of crops, along with such cultural and welfare projects as rural electrification, construction of standard houses and water facilities, and communication and methane gas facilities.

By the end of 1973, about 70 % of the government-set target was accomplished in farm road maintenance, while improvement of village streets and construction of small bridges reached 91 and 98 %, respectively.
- Improvement of roofs reached 43 per cent while
- Construction of community laundry facilities and drains was 70 % of the national target.
- A total of 52 % of the rural households, moreover, were supplied electricity,
- 69 % of the villages had built town halls, and
- More than half had established water supplycilities.

During the first four years of Saemaul Undong, 1970-1974, more than 60 % of government-fixed targets for major environmental changeshad been accomplished.During the first two years of the Movement, 1970-72, the government'sthe principle of helping villages that help themselves. strategy was to give priority assistance to the superior villages, based on The incentive was established for inferior villages to complete self-help projects in order to earn assistance from the government. This competitive strategy essentially remains, but in 1973 the government gave 500 bags of cement and one ton of reinforcing steel to each of the undeveloped villages to spur their processes of development.Despite substantial government assistance, however, the great bulk of the New Community Movement was claimed by the government to have been funded by the villagers, themselves. Of a cumulative total of approximately $306 million expended, according to 1974 government figures, the government had contributed less than one-third, with the remainder contributed by villagers. But the manner by which villagers contributed is not clear.

Indeed, the Movement was considered so successful by government authorities, that they encouraged its spread to urban communities for the uplift of city life. Government figures for 1974 reveal a cumulative expenditure over $22,00,000, or almost 87 % of the total, with government contributing approximately 13 % only.

The activities of urban Saemaul Undong include; community projects such as helping neighbors, improvement of streets, aforestation of urban spaces; family activities such as increasing savings, betterment of living conditions, consumer protection; office activities such as improvement of management and services, frugal use of materials; and school activities such as the improvement of study attitudes, linkages between schools and the community, and school services for the community. Participation has been impressive. By 1974, for example, about 5.9 million family members and 45 thousands schools were reported to have participated in the urban New Community Movement.Popular awareness of the Movement was enhanced by the government when, in November 1975.

President Park himself composed the "Song of Saemaul,".

The first lines are:

Dawn bell tolls,
New dawn breaks;
Let us get up, you and me,
O build the new community.
(To be sung "vigorously and cheerfully")

Although the government has endeavored to spread the Movement to urban areas, rural development remains the emphasis. To boost rural income, the government has sought to export urban industriliazation to the villages by establishing Saemaul factories as sources of major off-farm income. Thus, some villagers can be employed in factories at times other than planting and harvesting seasons. Usually located in suburban and rural areas near cities or towns, the government supports these factories by subsiding materials. By 1974, the construction of 311 factories was completed, offering about 30,000 villagers new jobs. An additional 200 are planned for completion by the end of 1975. Although the government's goal is a total of 770 Saemaul factories, a number of factories have failed.

The income of farmers and fishermen is reported to have increased dramatically in recent years compared to the income of urban laborers-according to government statistics-from 60 % of urban laborers' income in 1967, to 90 % in 1973. The greatest increase was registered in the first four years of Saemaul Undong, from 1970 to 1973-a jump from 67% to 90%. Indeed, the latest statistics for 1975 show that the average family income of farmers and fishermen now surpass that of urban laborers-$1,863 compared to $1,757, or 106 % of the latter. The fact that the average family income of farmers and fishermen has increased at a faster than that of urban laborers may be attributed partly to rural-to-urban migration which, by decreasing the number and size of rural families, effects an increase in average rural family income. However, the fact that the great increase was registered from the inception of Saemaul Undong a jump from 67.5 % in 1970 to 106 % in 1975 leads to the conclusion that the Saemaul Movement provided the main energy for the economic uplift of rural life. The government's projection is to achieve an average rural family income of $3,500 by 1981. Meanwhile, the government expects to achieve self-sufficiency in rice production in 1978, ostensibly ending Korea's dependency on rice imports.

Continuing Support

As suggested above, rural development programs in Asia, and elsewhere, can be characterized as either predominantly decentralized or centralized-namely the so-called community development approach, or an approach deriving from national economic development plans. The former places primary emphasis on local autonomy in rural communities. The latter treats central and local government institutions as the main agencies of rural development.Both approaches have incurred frequent criticism, especially when attempts are made to develop rural areas in developing countries. The community development approach fails to enhance rural development when the subject is not equipped with adequate financial resources and efficient personnel with needed technological ability. In this case, local autonomy might accelerate regressive tendencies and thus bring about increased central control of local administration. On the other hand, approaches deriving from national economic development plans tend to encourage highly centralized governmental control of every aspect of rural life which, in turn, tends to alienate the positive support of rural residents. They then become more dependent on the government and hence less creative. Local initiative becomes stifled and voluntary participation becomes minimal.In the 1960's, the Korean government adopted the economic development plans approach whereby all rural development programs were dominated and controlled by a highly centralized government. Korea is the inheritor of the Confucian tradition of a highly hierarchical government authority structure, with lower levels of government functioning as communication channels implemented by a unidirectional process from top to bottom. The hierarchy ran from the President's office through the ministries, provinces, countries, towns or townships, to the villages or cities. In theory, at least, all local officers were appointed by the central government, and little local autonomy existed.At the base of the hierarchy in rural areas was the Ri (village) chief, appointed by the central government from among residents of each village, and members of the Ri development committee selected from among villagers approved by the Ri chief who served as its chairman. The main function of the Ri chief and his committee was to implement national plans for village development in terms of village security, women's activities, and production. In this highly centralized setting, however, rural residents were either indifferent to development plans or behaved dysfunction ally with respect to the committee's efforts.Given this counterproductive situation, the government had three general options open for organization adjustment which, in retrospect, can be postulated.

* First is the integrative type of program designed to be country wide in scope and to replace the existing administrative organization with a new one through which technical and financial resources can be channeled to achieve centrally planned development goals.
* Second is the project-type program limited in geographic scope to certain parts of a country and designed as a testing ground for techniques and practices.

* Third is the adaptive-type program which is country-wide in scope but involves some change in administrative organization. It seeks to impart financial and technical support of government to the tasks of stimulating community self-help.

  It is this third approach that formed the strategy for Saemaul Undong. It combines government initiatives, technical assistance, and financial support with local self-determination and self- help decision making, on a nation-wide basis, and has occasioned some change in government organization.The leaders of the New Community Movement are not government bureaucrats, but so called Saemaul leaders who are responsible for putting the Movement into practice in their respective villages and work places. In each of the 34,665 rural villages, in all the Dongs (urban districts) in 35 cities, and in small and large communities, the Saemaul leaders are the key figures responsible for leading the Movement and working with the people.In each village, Saemaul leaders comprise one man and one woman popularly elected, and replaceable at any time, by the village assembly which consists of one elector from each village household. The Saemaul woman leader is usually in charge of women's activities. The Saemaul-leader has replaced the Ri chief, as chairman of the reconstituted village development committee, but the position of Ri chief has been retained.The most dramatic if not revolutionary change in organization for rural development is the creation of the position of Saemaul leader who, since he is elected and removable by his neighbors, is responsible to them, rather than to the Ri chief and other appointed government officials. One should be hard pressed to find a better example of the adaptive-type program. The Saemaul leader is responsible for tapping the well-spring of hope, aspiration, and enthusiasm of the villagers and to lead them toward self-fulfillment.One might surmise that a Saemaul leader would have to be motivated by compassion, altruism or self-sacrifice, precisely because he receives no pay from either the government or the villagers. Aside from the satisfaction of improving his village life and surrounding, one may ask what incentives exist for a villager to become a Saemaul leader?The government offers a number of incentives to Saemaul leaders. The Saemaul leader does not always have to communicate through the Ri chief, upward through the normal channels of the government hierarchy. If he has a special problem, he may communicate directly with the provincial governor and ministers. The government also may provide financial help for the education of sons and daughter of Saemaul leaders. A leader who does an exceptional job may receive honorific awards from government officials, even including recognition by President Park, and such a leader can be offered a government position. Saemaul leaders who travel for official purposes will be given discounts on travel rates. And, finally, the government can give loans to deserving leaders, as distinguished from other villagers.Projects are managed jointly by the Saemaul leader, the Ri chief and township officials. There is little chance for abuse or corruption, as all records are open to the villagers. Moreover, the government's financial support normally is in the form of raw materials such as cement and steel for construction rather than in the form of funds.Plans and programs are formulated through the village development committee with the Saemaul leader usually exercising the initiative, or otherwise taking an active role in program planning as committee chairman. Village plans and programs are then reviewed and adjusted by councils to township, country, provincial and national levels.

Evaluation

It is apparent that, from the perspectives of most villagers and the government, the Korean rural development program is an ongoing success. The government repeatedly points with pride-in a number of successive publications, in Presidential addresses and statements, in news releases, and by other means-to surprising achievements already through a so-called voluntary, self-help, grass-roots democracy that is represented as SouthKorea's answer to NorthKorea's communist system. But obvious successes should not obscure incipient and potential problems.
One of these problems is inherent conflict between the appointed Lee chief and the elected Saemaul leader. If the Lee chief's administrative power supersedes that of the Saemaul leader, participation of villagers maybe negated or reduced.Insofar as a Saemaul leader may exercise his discretion to bypass the Lee chief and other intervening government officials to confer directly with higher ranking authorities, he is likely to ignore the role of the Lee chief in the village. And insofar as the Saemaul leader is successful in his leadership role, villagers will also tend to ignore the lee chief. Since they elect the Saemaul leader, they are disposed to follow his advice while suspecting the ability and authority of the Lee chief who is directly appointed by the government.One way to resolve this conflict is to combine the functions and positions of Saemaul leader and Lee chief, in effect by abolishing the latter position and transferring its powers to that of the elected Saemaul leader. The key question here is the whether the Saemaul leader could be induced to undertake such extra duties and responsibilities without financial inducement. Surely, the spirit of self-sacrifice that supposedly motivates the unpaid, but pivotal Saemaul leader, might be lost were he to receive the pay of the Lee chief. Perhaps this spirit could be salvaged by paying the Saemaul leader only a portion of the former Ri chief's pay.It would be unprecedented and uncharacteristic, however, for the government to vest the appointed Ri chief's authority and responsibilities in the position of the elected Saemaul leader. After all, the Saemaul movement was designed, initiated, and managed by the government. Participation in the movement is

not completely voluntarily, as the government exercises its authority to grant or withhold subsidies to villages on condition of such participation. Moreover, the government on occasion utilizes coercion to assure support for the movement. The government's authority in this movement is clear and unchangeable.Nevertheless, having introduced a Korean-style democracy at the village level, the government may have embarked on an irreversible course of systemic change whereby the rural populace may come to demand popular election or selection of not only the Ri chief but of other government officials as well who are now appointed. It is highly unlikely that any future government could reverse this new Korean-style democracy.It may be too early to assess the significance of initiating village democracy in a highly centralized political system, some form of which Korea here to fore always has experienced. How far can"altruism and self-sacrifice" be pushed without basic institutional change? How much can be accomplished by an ideological approach without changes in the institutional structure of rural society? Has the government unwittingly planted seed that may grow to challenge its authority and stability? Or will village democracy actually enhance national unity and security? These are not rhetorical or abstract questions. They are questions arising from the conflicting positions of the Saemaul leader and Lee chief.

Another problem consists of achieving rural development on a regional, area, or inter-village basis. Currently, each village is expected to draft, with the assistance and guidance of government officials and specialists from various ministries, a five-year development plan which will be coordinated with plans for other villages, so that area and regional plans will be made for such improvements as feeder roads, rural electrification, reforestation, land reclamation, irrigation, drainage, and flood control. But these will be regional and area plans devised and imposed by government officials, rather than by villagers, themselves. Necessary infrastructure, moreover, for inter-village cooperation is lacking for the establishment of regional centers for the location of common warehouses, storage, milling, marketing, credit, and farm machinery facilities; for maternity, child-care, and medical facilities; and for agricultural extension, education, and library facilities that could serve a number villages. Implementation of area and regional development plans will require cooperation among villages which, because of the nature of Saemaul Undong, will be difficult to achieve. That is to say that the government has pursued a strategy to promote competition, not cooperation, among villages. It has rewarded successful villages, over others, in order to induce undeveloped villages to earn through self-help government subsidies. And the government has established the goal for all villages to become developed by 1981.The government's effort to advance rural development has been on a village, not a regional,basis this nuclear village-approach, although producing noteworthy successes, paradoxically may thwart inter-village cooperation. As villages become developed and achieve a certain level of common property and individual wealth, their inhabitants may become less inclined to integrate their efforts cooperatively with those of less advanced or less prosperous villages in inter-village or regional rural development programs.Korea's Saemaul Undong is dramatically changing the Korean countryside and improving rural life. It is unique, indigenous, and thus far successful. But as the government enters the next phases of rural development and of increasing agricultural productivity, it would do well to study- and profit by- the experience of other countries.There is no dispute that the rapid economic development in Korea since the early 1970's owes largely to the massive rural reconstruction drive called the "Saemaul Movement" initiated by the late President Park Chung-hee in 1970.Korea's ambitious industrialization programs which was started in the early 1960's would not have been a success, had they not been accompanied by the modernization of its rural areas for which the Saemaul Movement was responsible.By the time the nation's second economic development plan was drawing to a close in 1970, it was realized that whereas the industrialization programs were going relatively smoothly, the nation's 20 million farmers', roughly two-thirds of the entire population, were still living in poverty. Therefore the gap in living standard of rural and urban population only widened. The problems facing agricultural areas in Korea were not so much due to the poor living conditions of its farming population but their declining morale. Finding themselves in life-long poverty, the majority of farmer's lives with a sense of helplessness which makes many of them to search for opportunities to move out to cities. This does not mean to say that there weren't many technological problems to solve in Korean agricultural. First of all, farming in Korea, still being carried out mostly by hands on tiny patches of lands owned by individual farmers, had to be modernized to make sure better efficiency and productivity. However, for the modernization of farming, farming units would have to be made bigger and doing this involved enormous problems including breakup of the existing small, individual land ownerships to be replaced by shared ownerships or abandoning the traditional values and social morals which were held over the years.The Saemaul Movement in its early stage, therefore, had to put emphasis on changing the farmers' old fashioned way of thinking. The first and foremost task was on how to put confidence, hope and, above all, a new sense of value stressing the need for cooperative labor in the minds of farmers. Furthermore, they had to be persuaded that they could lead a better life only if they adopted "new ways" as recommended by the Saemaul Movement. Thus, the motors of the movement were, "Diligence, Self-help and Cooperation" and "We Too Can Live Better" and "We Can Also Do It!"

The government started the movement by selecting and promoting "model villages" in each region of the country with a budget approximately equivalent to two billion U.S dollars, which would be used over the next five years. In addition to modernizing their farming on enlarged farmlands, these villages were talks into tearing down their outdated thatched houses to replace them with new Government-designed "model farmhouses," and building or expanding the roads, bridges and dykes in their neighborhoods. They were at the same time encouraged, with loans given in most cases, to develop new non-farming secondary income sources by way of raising live stocks or rare plants and flowers that could be marketed in efforts to increase their income. The idea was to show to the rest of the farming communities that they could do the same by copying these model villages. The results were contagious as intended, leading to the success of the Saemaul Movement in its initial stage.The average annual farm household income, which stood at a meagre $747 in 1970 when the movement started, increased to $4,450 in 1979, nearly a six-fold increase in less than a decade. The success of the movement is shown not only by this and other impressive statistics, but also by the fact that today one can no longer find the old-fashioned housings built mostly by a combination of straws and mud in any farming community in Korea.The assassination of President Park Chung-hee n 1979, however, plunged the Saemaul Movement into a serious crisis. As it has been seen, the Saemaul Movement from the outside was not only almost entirely Government-led, but also personally identified with the late President. After the death of the strong-man who was so personally involved with the movement, it was widely taken for granted that his death meant the end of the movement. Especially many intellectuals, who had looked at the movement with a cynical eye out of their hatred to Park's strong rule, predicted openly that the movement will and with the assassinated President for good.Perhaps the Saemaul Movement might have met the predicted fate, were it not for one of its strong, faithful supporters.The Headquarters of Saemaul Movement as a center for the civilian-led national movement comprises of eight member organizations, and 13 provincial chapters and 231 county level chapter offices under the direct control of the Headquarters. Those 8-member organizations were;

- Central Saemaul Leader's Association which has the members of 160,000 village leaders throughout the country,
- Central Federation of Saemaul Women's Clubs that has member units of more than 10,000 business and public organizations,
- Factory Saemaul Headquarters which consists of 16,200 factories, - - - Central Federation of Saemaul Youth Society that has members of 700,000 young men and women,
- Saemaul Library Headquarters that has 35,000 small libraries, - Saemaul Sports Association that has 7-sports clubs such asclubs of soccer, volleyball, badminton, cycling, tennis, baseball and hapkido marshal art, and lastly,

- Saemaul mini-Bank Association which has more than 4,000 village banks and its deposit amounts up to $1.5 billion as of April 1985.In supporting elements;
- Saemaul Research Institute and
- Federation of Saemaul Professors

In addition, 113 Saemaul Training Centers were conducting various training courses that also attain to results of more than 3 million people trained a year including 300 foreigners every year. Also Saemaul Newspaper Company is producing seven different kinds of periodicals which is used for publicity and training material.In conjunction with those activities, a number of long-term goals were set for the renovation and expansion of the Movement, which included a Saemaul fund of 50 billion won (equivalent to $600 million) which would be set up by 1988 to enable the Movement to achieve its financial independence, strengthening and expanding the existing Saemaul credit facilities established to provide loans to needy farmers, and vast expansion of training programs for the " Saemaul Leader," who are chosen to play leading, inspiring roles in each of the farming villages they live in.In order to get rid of the problems the Saemaul Movement has started a number of programs and project including one called the "program of searching and developing second-generation farmers and fishermen." Under this program a total of 11,000 young men and women have been selected and trained throughout the country for the last four and half years..

This young men and women, besides the special training they undergo, are given constant encouragements to live in their native communities. For instance, each of them receives 7 million won(over $8,600)in subsidy to spend for his campaign to improve farming in his community or neighborhood, and a considerable number of them are expected to be selected for trips to Japan and Taiwan to observe farming and fisheries industry in those countries.(The Saemaul Movement has sent a total of 3,400"Saemaul Leaders" abroad on similar tours for the last four and a half years.) Saemaul Headquarters in Seoul is also engaged in research and studies with the aim of developing a distribution system linking farmers and fishermen directly with the consumers throughout the country in connection with universities in Korea and Japan.There can be no questioning that it largely owes to the Saemaul Leaders that today the Saemaul Movement in Korea is not only alive and well, but being carried out more vigorously thanover.The facts are broadly known in the Korean communities that the Saemaul Movement is a unique way for the well-being of the Korean people who have been in hardship and poverty throughout Korea's 5,000-year history.Saemaul leaders of Saemaul Movement in Korea will not stop striving every day of the year along with many people until they can better the national fate and create prosperous societies of their father land.

However, the meanings of the Saemaul Undong were so significant because of its consistent success, popularity, and strong support of the top political leadership, the term "Saemaul" tended to be used too often and too wide regardless the relation with Saemaul Undong. Therefore, in order to maintain the original image and influence of the Saemaul Undong, the word "Saemaul" should not be abused by either the government or private entities.

2. Comparison of Development Strategies

As mentioned earlier, development depends much on the leaders. One can find the evidence by comparing the characteristics of the three cases in terms of economic development. Table 13 shows that technology development and improvement of marketing are effective for rural development.

Table 13. Comparison of Development Strategies

Area (No. of Ri)	Changsori(1)		Kuokmal(8)	Bulwonri(1)
Farmland/ Household (ha.)	0.7		1.1	0.7
Main Crop	Scallion		Rice	Melon
Initiation of Development	1962		1973	1977
Core of Strategy	Technology Innovation, Cooperative Marketing		Spiritual Renovation	Innovation, Cooperative Marketing
Marketing Channels		Wholesale Market	Rural Market Middleman, etc.	Auction ('84) Wholesale Market ('85)
Village Level	1/286		Average : 95.5/286	12/286
Growth Rate ('83/82)	5.6 %		5.6 %	22.2 %

Judging from these tabulated figures, it is clear that technological innovation and successful marketing schemes are paramount tasks to pursue for practical socio-economic development.Leadership and spiritual renovations were key factors in the role of Saemaul Undong in rural development, but by far the most beneficial change in the standard of living was achieved by the innovation of marketing through village cooperation. Therefore, the Saemaul Undong's effort to modernize marketing schemes has produced the greatest overall effect.

From the comparison of the three case studies involved, we learned that successful socio-economic development of a community depends to the largest extent on the role of the village leaders in choosing proper strategies.Definitely, the village leader is responsible for making the choice among alternative strategies. So the failure to choose a path which effectively loosen the constraints imposed by the resource endowments, can depress the whole process of agricultural and economic development.In conclusion, exploration of new farming technologies and proper marketing of farm products are the most essential means to facilitate agricultural development. Each and every farmer and village leader attempt to boost economic opportunities for their village. However, not all are successful. Failure was caused not by the lack of resource endowments but by poor resource allocation. To elaborate, the choice of the most efficient path is more crucial to economic prosperity than the size of farmland.

As more and more farmers of Korea become acquainted with technical know-how any cash crop is bound to cease to be acash crop when it is popularized to the maximum extent possible. Although this phenomenon threatens farmers of Changsori-1Ku, they need not fear that every farmer will have hens, those pioneers who begin early by tilling scantily farmland are able to accumulate capital and expand the size of their farmlands. The late comers, then are compelled to switch their efforts to other non-agricultural development processes.

In spite of the small size of individual farmland, the enhancement of the farmers' educational level serves as a catalyst in the illumination of the delay lag in their farming know-how for agricultural modernization.

V. Saemaul Education

1.Philosophy and Method of Saemaul Education

 The Saemaul Education has been recognized as one of the educational institutions not only in the Korea but also in the world, which has played so important role in the Saemaul Undong. Most of the people from the top to grass root knew well what the Saemaul education is. They have been educated by the Saemaul training programs so that the majority of them could be fully motivated to participate in the Saemaul Undong. Its contribution has been recognized by sevaral Asian and African countries such as Uganda, Vetnam, Myanmar, Laos. Their governments sent their officials to directly see the movement and learn some possible application.

Some Asian countries like Thailand and Malaysia invited the Saemaul trainers to provide the Saemaul education fortheir development agents and workers to learn Korean workmanship based Saemail Undong with the Saemaul spirit; diligence, self-help and cooperation.

The Saemaul education is all the educational and disciplinary activities of non-formal education which have been assigned as Saemaul education centers by the Ministry of Home Affairs(currently Ministry of Public Security Administration) such as;

- Saemaul Leaders Training Institute,
- Canaan Farmers School,
- Provincial famers training centers, and so on.

Method of Saemaul Education

 As well known the Saemaul Education has enhanced both of the potential and active participation of people. The education has affected people's full participation in the Saemaul Undong, so that the Saemaul education could surely be considered as one of the most important factors for the success of the movement. From the practitioner's point of view, the Saemaul education has been publicly recognized by the Ministry of Home Affairs (MHA) which is a national coordinating organization(GO) for the movement promotion, as one of major factors which made the Saemaul Undong successful. The Saemaul education could make all levels of people from the beginning to the top to fully participate in movement and to effectively promote the Saemaul projects in their respective area.In the 1980', Headquarters of Saemaul Undong was established, it also emphasized its educational function by way of putting up "Education and Training Division" in its organization set-up and Saemaul training buildings either in its compound or in the vicinal towns, and now the Korea SaemaulUndong Center undertakes a variety of Saemaul education programs for thousands of trainees in a year and coordinates all the other Saemaul education programs.

In 1981 the Ministry of Home Affairs separately built the Saemaul nursery schools in rural remote villages and in urban low-income areas and expanded them on 1982 by integrating day care centers and seasonal day care centers during busy farming times. Those schools might also be considered as a part of Saemaul educational programs worked out by the efforts of the Saemaul women's clubs.

The Saemaul youth clubs originated from the 4-H club are also working mainly on education activities for the youths in a certain community.

From the above reviews, it is certain that the Saemaul non-formal education has been the basis of all and successful Saemaul activities and that it is an impetus of the Saemaul Movement- a motive power of Saemaul Undong.

Saemaul Education emphasizes spiritual enlightenment which encourages the desire for participation as well as techniques that provide the people with practical directions for projects. In order to strengthen this spiritual aspect, the following subjects were taught;

- Ideology,
- Leadership,
- The scientific way of life,
- The directions of economic development,
- The directions of the movement,
- The people's attitude,
- The national policy of reunification of the nation,
- The reunification policy of the nation, and
- National history are taught on one hand.

On the other hand, for the technical aspects of the training, the following subjects were taught;

- General farm management,
- Cash crop production,
- Cattle husbandry,
- Silkworm culture,
- Swine and chicken breeding,
- Afforestation,
- Erosion control work,
- Agricultural civil engineering and
- Farm machinary .

The Saemaul Leader's Training Institute, opened in 1972, is the central training center of the country. It trained between 1973-79 a total of 40,539 trainees; 02,996 Saemaul leaders, 8,156 women Saemaul leaders, 9,802 leaders of society's top echelon – top leaders of society, 1,517 members of universities student committees, and 5,068 staff members of agricultural and fisheries organizations. In 1980, about 9,000(5,000 in regular courses and 4,000in special courses)

2. Main Courses and Modules

There are three main courses in Saemaul training:
(1). the course for Saemaul leaders,
(2). the course for women Saemaul leaders, and
(3).the course for social leadersincluding officials, business managers, intellectuals, and other influentials in the society.In any course of training the following three specific features are commonly stressed.

1) presentation of the experiences of successful village Saemaul leaders (case studies) are a very effective and persuasive means if educating other Saemaul and social leaders. For a member of the social elite, who makes policies for others to follow, the story of a poverty-stricken village woman, who, with no formal education, finally managed, through hard work, to overcome herself from poverty, and is now helping other villagers to live better, gives a long-lasting impression and makes him feel that the village woman is perhaps contributing much more to society than he is. By listening to such stories, the prominent person reevaluates his past life style and begins sincerely to respect the village Saemaul leaders, and therefore becomes better able to offer as much support to the village leaders as possible.

2) the training emphasizes **doing** rather than **talking**. All trainees live under the same conditions, eat the same food, make their own beds, and clean their living quarters. All sessions start exactly on time and end on time. All trainees participate in the morning jogging. No one expects special treatment. Everyone is treated equally. A thrifty life is practiced with no coffee or alcohol but only a simple diet composed mainly of coarse grains. Through such practices, the trainees learn that doing is much more difficult than talking and that the farmer's rough hands covered with calluses are more beautiful than the slim and pale hands of the lip server.

3) self-evaluation through group discussion makes the trainee evaluate ones past life style. The evaluation focuses on what one has done in the past and what one should do in the future;

(1) as a person,
(2) as the head of a family,

(3) as the head of an office, and
(4) as a leader in a society.

It is emphasized that one should think mainly about what he or she should do, not what others should do.The education period and contents are not fixed but rather, flexible in accordance with the specific needs of trainees and upon suggestion of institutions related to the Saemaul Undong. However, there is some uniformity in subject matter, discipline, successful case presentation, group discussion, meditation, and the other methodology of the education. Usually, education for Saemaul leaders is given for two weeks and that for leaders of society require one week period. In every course, most emphasis is placed on practical experience for the mental and behavioral change of trainees. The subjects commonly required in every course are:

-Philosophy and spirit of the Saemaul Undong (Saemaul Movement and national development).
-Direction of the Saemaul Undong for the specific year,
-National security and the international situation,
-Introduction to economic development,
-Natural conservation,
-Energy saving campaign,
-Public ethics and morality,
-Presentation of successful cases,
-Study tour to model project villages and panel discussion.

Several subject-matters are additionally offered in order to meet the needs of a specific group of trainees. For instance, the subject-matter taught to rural leaders is mainly technical, focusing on income boosting projects. Urban people learn how to improve business management and neighborhood relations, and women leaders usually learn child care, health care, and alternatives for economizing daily living.Some institutes undertake special short-term Saemaul education for those who cannot affords a long term. And two-or three-day-long refresher courses are also provided for alumni so they may renew their friendships and rearm themselves with a fresher Saemaul spirit.Saemaul education has already developed greatly as a social education program, supporting the expectation that it will continue in the future. The methods of education are quite different from those of formal education in many ways. The new approaches used in education have even been adopted by some regular schools.It is a common principle that trainees are collected at the campus with no connection nor communication with outside permitted. Trainees and trainers lodge together, eating at the same table, using the same facilities, and treating each other on just the same level. They create a blood-tied relationship to which they dedicate themselves in order to find the ideal way of life based upon truth and good will.Saemaul education won't emphasize sophisticated theories of research, instead, it calls for the steady and sincere practice and experiencing of what one think should be done. Each trainee gets up early in the morning, cleaning one's own bed, saluting to the national flag, singing the national anthem together, jogging together, practicing physical exercise together, carrying and cleaning one's own dishes, meditating by oneself under the broadcast of awakening the tainted people, listening to lectures presented by instructors including poor and ill-educated living heroes from the bottom class of the society, exchanging humble experiences with group or panel members, visiting the real sites of touching struggle against hardships, and above all fighting against oneself so as to lead oneself to an inner sanctuary remodeling oneself into a dedicated contributor to the common welfare.Success cases presented by community leaders in the rural tongue used to move most of the trainees, well-educated and ill-educated, young and old, men and women. Some stories are presented in movies or ppt.In order to understand the uniqueness of Saemaul education and methodology, it is useful to review its daily schedule in the course.

The Saemaul leaders arrive at the institute on Sunday afternoon from all over the country and register upon arrival. After registration, daily necessities such as a uniform and text materials are supplied. Then the trainees are divided into groups of several trainees per each room, and shown the dormitory where they will live during the period. The trainees settle into their accommodations and change into uniforms.They are then shown to classrooms to answer a background questionnaire and write a brief essay on what they feel about the education. The results of the background questionnaire are then carefully analyzed and taken into consideration in formulating the course. Once these entry procedures are completed, the trainees are invited to the cafeteria for dinner. Here they learn table etiquette related to group eating. The trainees wait in line for their food. After the meal they carry their trays and plates to the designated place for proper disposition.After dinner, trainees gather in the auditorium for an orientation session on what they should expect during the education period. All of the full time instructors live with the trainees. Next, a film strip is used to introduce the curriculum and daily schedule. Then the dormitory supervisor explains the life in the dormitory in detail. Preparing them thus to make mutual concessions for a conducive cooperative living, the trainees are able step into the "₩learn through living together." Finally, the trainees join in singing whole-some and joyful song under the music instructor's direction. The day ends with a roll call at 22:00.This roll call checks that everything is in order at the end of the first busy day.For the remainder of the training program of one to two weeks, the daily schedule is very tight. The Saemaul songs wake the trainees at 5:00 every morning and shortly thereafter they assemble your side. After a brief morning call, they jog and then undertake physical exercises. Following they return to the dormitory, they wash and clean up the facilities until breakfast at 07:00. At 08:00 all the trainees gather in the auditorium, where they meditate and sing the Saemaul songs together and then a volunteer among the trainees presents his or her experiences on the Saemaul programs of his or her village. Morning classes start at 09:00 and last four hours.The trainees are allowed one and half hours for lunch and relaxation.This is followed by afternoon classes ending at 18:100 after dinner, the trainees meet again to participate in group discussions for three hours until 22:00.This is immediately followed by a brief evening roll call with the trainees retiring at 22:30, unless further discussion is required.

As of 2009, there are many programs for foreigners i.e. one week program for the trainees from the Philippines, Tanzania, and Uganda was provided by Korean Saemaulundong Center from March 22 to March 2.

Those programs had started with disciplinary delegates from abroad as a chain of economic cooperation between Korea and foreign counties. The purpose of the program is to educate and convince the leaders of rural community development of the related countries and promote the international cooperation through the spirit of Saemaul Undong: diligence, self-help and cooperation. Hundreds of disciplines from dozens of countries have joined in the program and finished the course with success every year.

This training program had consequently brought about the senses on the necessity of Seamaul Undong for the developing countries through physical experience from success cases of actual community development leaders and showed them the fundamental character of Saemaul Undong thorough training and education. It also devoted for the participants to understand deeply about Korean's way of thinking and culture in broad aspect.

Evaluation, Monitoring and Feedback

Considering globalization and multi-culture both of domestic and abroad, Saemaul Undong should find its new role expectation.

In short, the Korean model of Saemaul Undong is in a transitional stage should take the shape of effective institutionalization, socialization and internalization, with desirable norms, structures and behavior cultivated by the movement in the globalized multi-culture society.

In the evaluation, there are three stages in the case of the Saemaul Leaders Training Institute:

(1) need assessment,

(2) intermediate monitoring, and

(3) assessment of education accomplishment.

The need assessment of trainees

It is made upon their arrival at the institute on Sunday afternoon in terms of their background, their knowledge of and attitude toward Saemaul Undong and needs and expectation from their prospective guidelines for better training and in slightly adjusting the subject-matter during instructor's meeting on morning. The intermediate monitoring and evaluation are made by trainers who stay with trainees at the same dormitory and who are in charge of different group discussions. Before going to bed, they exchange information and views about the trainees' attitude. The problem encountered can then be easily adjusted at a meeting if necessary which may be called as late as midnight. At the final session just before the closing ceremony, the trainees are asked to fill out a questionnaire on the training programs which is concerned with two main items: what the Saemaul Undong is and, what it changed in their way of thinking, if anything. In addition, the results of the group discussion are analyzed to assess the training effect. Under the proposition that the crucial effect of the training depends upon the trainees' actual role in their field and community life. A variety of follow-up activities are also considered important. There are four kinds of follow-up programs for the trainees;

The first follow-up action;
 The communication through letters from trainees, the director and trainers, encouraging them to write about what they are doing and describe what problems they may have faced with. The Saemaul Leaders Training Institute publishes several booklets upon Saemaul Undong. Its contents mainly concerns successful cases and letters from and between trainees
.

The second follow-up action;
 The trainer's visit to trainees' homes all over the country.

The third follow-up action;
 A one day session at the county level which is convened by the institute in order to encourage the trainees to keep in-formed on Saemaul projects in other areas and to solve the problems they have faced with.

The last follow-up action;
 The trainer's attendance at the alumni meeting. This is voluntarily held in the form of a room-mate, session-mate or other kind of small group gathering where alumni exchange information and love.

VI. Achievements and Role of SaemaulUndong for MDGs

1. Achievement and Successful Factors

As of 2010, the 40th year of Saemaul Undong since 1970, Chosun Daily Newspaper reported that about 95% of Korean point out the natioal development of Korea depended mostly on Saemaaul Undong.

Through the Saemaul Undong, Korean rural society has been remarkably improved. The people could enjoy a modernized convenient life, having escaped from the former unsanitary and uncomfortable surroundings early in the 1970's. What is more important than among others is that Saemaul Undong has inspired the people to have self-confidence and strong will full of self-help and cooperative spirit. This effect seems to have resulted from visible and tangible outcomes and changes. Most farmers have been equipped with
capability of planning and realizing better quality of life. The villagers still have lots of things to do in some fields, but it is believed that they can do better without repeating trial and errors that they have made before. Major priority of
the Saemaul projects in the country side in the future will be laid on an inter-community program that covers several vicinal villages as a performer as well as beneficiary. Such a new pattern of program will be focused on the arrangement of comfortable and convenient life space at an inter-community level, as regional development rather than village level development is socioeconomically urgent. Accordingly effects of village level project should be interrelated and contributed to the regional development. The Saemaul Undong has followed new phases since 1981 when it was again vitalized at the initiative of non-governmental organization. The Headquarters of Saemaul Undong, functioning as a key station of various central and local private organization, has taken over major responsibilities with regard to the implementation of the movement from the government. It is the very intention of the government that the Saemaul Undong as a nationwide movement should be entirely undertaken by private sector. The Saemaul Undong in the future will give much emphasis on the social development aspect. When the people's income level gets higher and more people get enlightened, their concerns about and demand for sociocultural development will be sure the grow greater. Even though the Saemaul Movement itself is certainly a synthetic concept of culture, it will work as a motive to give birth to newer culture of higher dimension.
This book deals mostly with some of important aspects which might be transferable to other developing countries. Major concentration has been focused on the aspects of the process of initiation on community development

programs, effective roles played by combined efforts both GO's and NGO's, and operational structures and leadership and so on.

1). Lessons

According to the experiences of Saemaul Undong, so far, the following would be available to be considered:

(1).Community development movement needs to consider the historical, traditional background, since the mentality of people of each country as a whole has been extensively influenced by their traditional value system.

In particular values and attitudes had a serious effectto social development because of its tendency to emphasize one's moral obligations and formulate labor force. There are many things to be rectified in the structure of the Korean consciousness, such as egoistic attachment and exclusionism rooted in traditional oriental ideas, nihilism, and the formalism and selfishness influenced by western individualism. The Saemaul Spirits and the Undong are in part to remove such an irrational and unhealthy system of value and way of living and thereby establish a sound and productive order in the community.

(2).Saemaul projects were classified into three categories such as environmental improvement, income increas and spiritual enlightenment.

Environmental improvement projects are designed for villagers to improve unscientific or unsanitary surroundings of community with their own efforts so as to create a convenient and cheerful atmosphere proper for welfare life. Improve living surroundings have given a sort of will and self-assurance to villagers. Without visual and direct benefit from the initial project, a developmental spirit could not be generated by the villagers. So the improvement of community environment must be an initial priority program.

(3).Projects need to be chosen by the consensus of community people, Saemaul projects are selected at village meetings and carried out with the participation of the majority of villagers.

Development committees prepare project plans and execute them after the approval at village meeting.
Such projects should benefit all community members instead of specific persons only. The profits gained from the projects should be returned equally to all participants. Also projects must contribute to enhance production and income directly or indirectly. Otherwise, villagers would hesitate to participate continuously.

(4).Projects should be guided by elected community leaders. Saemaul leaders play a pivotal role in selection and execution of projects.

There are two Saemaul leaders in each village, one male and one female. They are elected at village meeting depending on their trust and leadership regardless of their age and educational background. Saemaul leaders do not receive any remuneration from villagers or the government. They serve sacrificially for the development of the village where they live. When the villager's ability turns out sufficient for a specific project or when villagers face some difficult problems, the government provides matching financial and technical assistance.

Most of all the highest achievement of the Saemaul Undong is the acquirement by villagers of the self-assurance and the confidence that,"We can do it." Through the Saemaul Undong, efficient manners of life and rational ways of thinking have rooted among the people. The Saemaul spirit has become the new norm of conduct for the people. Economically also, the Saemaul Undong has played an important role in bringing on rapid growth. Korea has successfully tided over the difficulty of the oil crisis and pushed per capita GNP and export expansion.

In rural communities the three liberation movements;"free from the Chige(A-frame)", "free from lamp," and "free from straw roof" were launched at the initial stage of the movement. These achievements were evaluated as the innovative programs for better community life. All villages have become "developed" communities, and then looked forward to becoming "self-managing" "welfare" communities, the ideal type of community through Saemaul Undong. The movement in factories has conquered the economic recession. Smooth labor-management relationship can be forced by the movement, in which managers and workers discuss and solve problems in mutual dialogue and in which managers look after employees like their own family members. By participating in group discussion, workers can improve themselves in a rational and positive direction and exchange broad knowledge and experience on their work, thereby contributing much to productivity increase in the industrial sector.

The achievement and experiences gained in the 1970s will be comprehensively analyzed, so that the movement will be implemented more vigorously. Parallel with the forthcoming advent of an industrial society in the future, Korea faces the challenge to realize a justice society based on a sound value system and conduct a welfare state where development benefits can affect all the people. In socio-economic aspects, a further balance will be needed between growth and stability through the Saemaul Undong. The movement will be developed into a drive to create a society where in the midst of discrepancy between regions, and sectors, all the people can improve the quality of their lives. At the same time, the movement will be made a more scientific and rational movement, The Saemaul Undong can survive only when it develops, through overall social development and advancement of the consciousness of the people, into a voluntary participation based on science and rationality.

2). Lessons

The Saemaul Undong of Korea spreaded from farming villages to every corner of the country. It applied to factories and cities as well, where conditions are entirely different from those of farming villages. It would be impossible for factories and cities to merely follow or imitate the Saemaul Undong as it has been implemented in farming village. It should be developed into a creative movement through which the life of individuals is reformed and community life is improved on the strength of diligence, self-help and cooperation. Should we handle the farm economy merely from the viewpoint of material advantage? Should the Saemaul Undong vanish away in farming villages, the base of the movement, it might be difficult for the movement to spread cities and factories. 1f the Saemaul Undong is to penetrate factories and cities, the conditions of which differ entirely from those areas, in a new form, its theories should be synthesized and systemized. Saemaul Undong was not preceded by theories but the implementation could be able to adapt itself to other conditions in a creative way only through systemized theories. And without considerations, the Saemaul Undong could neither change now dominate the culture of life. No social movement can exercise a sustained influence if it cannot dominate the culture of life. Of course, many meaningful movements have achieved successful results through implementation lather than theories, as is the case with the Saemaul Undong.

But those movement have also been able to clarify their significance and exercise influence as history only when supported later by ideological studies. Nonetheless, the movement should be developed into a historical force that influences the people's life itself as a whole and steer the historic destiny of our country, transcending the socio-economic limitations counted on.

It is true that Korea has achieved a remarkable economic growth sufficient to draw world attention, and that our farming villages have begun rehabilitation, washing away the taint of chronic poverty The Saemaul Undong should be a nations-wide movement, but at the same time a drive led by those who are poor in spirit, those people who know the sorrow of poverty, who seek social justice and who are humble enough to harbor brotherly affection toward people living in misery. We always have to keep in mind, however, that socio-economic environments are required that make diligence, self-help and cooperation meaningful and possible, if all the citizens are to find worth in hard work, take neighbors in harmony. The Saemaul Undong is thus neither a drive designed merely to increase economic income, nor an educational drive aimed at reforming one's attitude to life.

From the above description of the ideology and contents, the main features of the Saemaul Undong can be summarized as follows.

(1) The movement was initiated by government, especially backed by the president. All levels of government, both central and local, were involved in the movement, and every rural village was affected by this movement. Such a massive participation and government support was probably unprecedented in the history.

(2) The Saemaul Undong was designed and implemented entirely around the individual village unit. The rural village is a naturally identified primary unit of community life characterized by the pursuit of common traditional interests.

(3) The Saemaul Undong does no differ much from other community development movements in the sense of pursuing materialistic betterment of rural society. But it does differ greatly from others in that spiritual enlightenment has been tightly combined, from the beginning, with materialistic aspects.

(4) The general procedure elsewhere in launching community development programs has been to build up ideology and formulate a plan with objectives and various strategies enunciated prior to actual implementation.

But in the case of the Saemaul Undong, it was only after an action was taken that an ideology and appropriate strategies were developed.

(5) A wide range of development activities represents another feature of the Saemaul movement. At the central level, almost all the government's programs related to rural development have been categorized under the Saemaul label.

Some criticisms were followed however much more positive evaluations has been found and the followings are accepted as effects of the Saemaul Undong:

- Through the successful completion of the projects as achievements, self-confidence was fostered.
- It awakened the grassroots' people to the importance of welfare and improvement of the quality of life.
- Through the active participation of villagers in the movement, social leadership and democratic citizenship were fostered.
- By installing the importance of labor for the enhancement of productivity, the self-supporting economy of the nation was strengthened.
- The movement greatly contributed to making the best use of available resources.
- The movement made a lasting contribution to raising the standard of living and economic growth of Korea and so on.

With focus on rural areas, the effect of the movement are summarized as follows:

- Enhancement of technical know-how;
- Self-sufficiency in rice production;
- Improvement on marketing methods;
- Increased the annual income of farming households;
- Positive change in farmers' attitudes; and
- Improved rural welfare.

Consequently, by nurturing the innate potential of the Korean people, the women boosted national strength for further acceleration of the socio-econom`ic development of Korea. As a result, the movement projects a positive image of Korea.The Saemaul Undong was launched under the government initiative. With government support aimed to improve farm income, massive investment projects were put into effect to build infrastructures. Unfortunately, after ten years of experience, the movement has become subjects of criticism mainly because of its top-down authoritarian performance pattern. In the course of its implementation, there emerged substantial evidences that the government-initiated approaches have hindered the voluntary participation of rural villagers in the drive and even led to the mass allocation of resources.

3). Key Factors of Successful Saemaul Undong

From the above review, studies and experiences of the authors, the followings are summarized as the key factors of successful Saemaul Undong.

(1)Leadership and Patriotism
- philosophy of the top leader
- attitude of "check-up the spot"
- passion and vision for the mother land
(2) Administrative Support and Strategy
- efficient administration from bottom to top level
- efficient strategy mobilizing extensive participation
- networks among all relevant organizations of Korea
(3)Local Official's Devotion
-personal devotion to the development of communities
-exclusive responsibility for guiding some specific fields
-provision of preliminary training for officials together with community leaders
-cooperation and networking between officials and community people
-personnel management according to official's personal achievement

(4) People's Awakening

-sustained intensive training of leaders from various fields

-provision of priority support for outperforming communities to stimulate self-competitiveness among the people

-public relation activities by mass media introducing newly found leaders or successful communities

-people's recognition of their own capabilities with regards to the environmental changes by themselves

(5) Community Leaders' Contribution

- villagers' selection of community leaders and intensive leadership training programs

- motivation of community member's participation encouraged by their leader's self-sacrifices

- encouragement of leaders with respect from the people and morale-strengthening policy of the government.

2. Prospect of 21st Century

Pictures in the year 2025

People born in 1900 could expect to live just more than 36 years. Today, the global average is over 65, and it is expected to exceed 72 by 2025. The century has seen dramatic changes in everything from medical care to literacy rates, and the changes will accelerate in the 21st century. Not all of them are desirable; the number of slum dwellers will sharply increase from 810 million in 1995 to an estimated 2.1 billion in 2025. But many things blessed- e-mail, cell phone, home automation-weren't even a distant dream one century ago. In 1950 there were just one city with a population of more than ten million - New York. In 1995 there were 380 and in 2025 there will be 650 with population of more than one million as shown in Table 14.

The urbanization will appear mainly in the developing countries of Asia, Africa and Latin America. Now more than two-thirds rural, will be half urban by 2025. The number of cities will be almost doubled in 2025 compared with those in 1995. As a result, rural residents fell from 55% in 1995 to 35% in 2025.

Regarding health, the number of medical doctor, phamacist and health care cost also will be continuously increased. Non-the less, AIDs related death and suicides will be increased too.

Except birth rate and infant mortality, the other indicators are mostly increased. Birth per woman and infant mortality will be tended to reduce from 3.17 and 5.9% in 1995 to 2.36 and 3.1%, respectively.

Considering the poor, quality of life in 2005 will be not so much enhanced. Urban poor and slum will be doubled within the same period. The number of people living in poverty is increased from 2400 million in 1995 to 3300 million in 2025.

Family and private life concerns, divorce rate per 1000 people is increased from 0.04 in 1995 to in 2025.

Adults literacyrate will increase from 55% in 1995 to 82% in 2025. In other words, the rest 18% in 2025 is illiterate.

Though the labor force grows unemployed also increases, too. Oil production per year, is prospected from 20 billion barrels to 30 billion barrels.

Table14. Prospect of 21st century

Cities	1995	2025
Pop, greater than 100,000	3,780	6,800
Pop. greater than 1 million	380	650
Urban residents, % of world	45%	61%
Rural residents, % of world	55%	39%
Urban poor, in millions	1,640	3,050
Urban slum	810	2,100
Illness and disease	1995	2025
People per doctor	3,780	2,500
People per pharmacist	11,154	8,500
Hospital beds, in mil.	18.2	23
Health-care costs, in billions	$2,500	$4,000
AIDS-related deaths, in millions	0,5	10
Suicides, in thousands	410	500
Deprivation IN MILLIONS	1995	2025
Living in poverty	2,400	3,300
Undernourished	1,800	500
Starvation-related deaths	20	10
Killed by dirty water	9.1	3.7
No adequate shelter	1,100	700
No access to medical care	1,500	700
Private life	1995	2025
Marriage rate per 1,000 people	4	5
Divorce rate per 1,000 people	.04	1
Births per woman	3.17	2.36
Household size, people	4.3	4.0
Contraceptive, use	56%	75%
Infant mortality, percent per year	5.9%	3.1%
Family income, in thousands	$13.4	$14.2
Death-to-birth ratio	1:2.8	1:2.3
Education	1995	2025
Percent of adults who are literate	55%	82%
Primary-school-educated adults, in billions	1.2	3.3
No access to schools, in millions	1,000	500
Public libraries, in thousands	270	500
Employment	1995	2025
In the labor force, in millions	1,900	2,500
Unemployed, in millions	100	200
People per device	1995	2025

Radios	3.2	1.7
Televisions	6.8	1.7
Daily newspapers, in thou.	699	1.214
Telephones	7.7	7.7
Fax machines	165.7	24.3
Videocassette recorders	11.6	4.3
Communication	1995	2025
E-mails sent, in billions	6	50
Internet users, in millions	18	80
Languages	9,500	8,000
Official state languages	95	150
Energy production	1995	2025
Oil, in billions of barrels per year	20	30
Nuclear power, in billions of kilowatt hours	630	1,000
Known nat. gas reserves in trillions of cu. m.	86	100
Transportation	1995	2025
Roads, in millions of miles.	17	25
Rail-passenger miles per year, in billions	1,100	2,000
Air-traffic-passenger miles per year, in billions	950	3,000

Source: Newsweek, Dec 27, 1999-Jan3, 2000

Hunger and Obesity

The majority underfed live in rural areas of developing countries and slums in developed countries as shown in Table15. Though the Asia-Pacific region has the largest absolute number of poor and food-insecurity people,the highest percentage is in Africa. Drought spreads hunger worldwide and armed conflicts are worsening food insecurities.

Hunger and malnutrition affect two groups. The first is preschool children: some 146 million are underweight because of malnutrition caused by mostly absolute poverty. Child hunger is frequently passed on from mothers who themselves are malnourished; about 20 million children are born underweight per year as shown in Table 16. Undernourished youngsters are inaccessibleto get even the most basic education. Malnutrition also delays or stops physical and mental growth. Most tragically, infectious disease such ad measles or whooping cough can kill undernourished children more readily than well-fed ones.

Although women are the main producer of food throughout the world, more than 60 % of the world's hungry are female. Traditionallywomen eat less than men do. Three hundred women die per day during childbirth by iron deficiency.

Table 15. Where are the underweight children?

Countries	in millions
India	57
Bangladssh	8
Pakistan	8
China	7
Nigeria	6
Ethiopia	6
Indonesia	6
Rest of the world	48
Total	146

Source: Scientific America, Sep. 2007

Table. 16 Where are the Low - Birth Weight Babies Born?

Regions	in million
South Asia	11.4
Sub-Sahara Africa	4.0
Asia	2.0
West Asia / North Africa	1.4
Latin America / Caribbean	1.1
Eastern Europe / former USSR	0.4
Total	20.3

Source: Scientific America, Sep. 2007

3.International Development Cooperation

Drastic shifts have takenplace in the last decade. The relationships between East and West, North and South(Have vs Have not) have dramatically been changed. However, these changes have brought not so much poverty alleviation in developing countries. In developing countries, in other words, in the Third World, more than one billion people remain in absolute poverty. As a result, eight million children die each year from preventable diseases and one-third of children in developing countries has physical or mental disorders brought about by malnutrition. On the other hand, one can easily find various and nutritious rations for pets such as dogs and cats in the United States of America, Japan and EU countries.

When we accept enhancing chance of life and quality of life, in other words, social welfare or social justice as the final goal of development in this global community, we should reduce the gap between North and South. From this point of view, each person in the economically highly-endowed countries devote just over seventy dollars a year through taxation on government overseas aid (Official Development Assistance: ODA). Of course, there are also various services provided by Non-Government Organizations (NGOs) besides ODA.

In the case of Korea, though the country itself is a developing one up to now, there have been increasing requests seeking aid from developing countries. They have requested for Korea's economic and technological cooperation. Recognizing the interdependency of the world economy, Korea has endeavored to fulfill its responsibilities to the global community by meeting such requests.

Korea's modern international cooperation program has launched since 1965. Just 15 years after Korean War which almost fully destroyed Korean peninsula, Korea has started returning her debt. Currently, the volume of Korea's international cooperation is not so huge, so far. However, the country will endeavor to realize the spirit of "Hongig Ingan", the foundation principle of Korea (to serve for the well-being of human beings) according to her development.

From the above aspect in mind, ODA of Korea will be reviewed for an effective international cooperation. Since, it is timely needed for more efficient ODA or NGOs activities of Korea. In essence, the purpose of this study is as follows:

-To review international aid in general;

-To review ODA of Korea;

-To provide alternatives strengthening international cooperation by mobilizing NGOs.

Types and Issues of International Cooperation

Types of international aid or international cooperation are classified differently by criteria such as characteristics of donors and types of aid, etc. However, types of aid are classified generally as follows:

-Grant Aid

Grant aid is the fund provided to developing countries without obligation of repayment. Hence, it can flexibly be used in various needs of the recipient countries. There are several kinds of grant aids such as a) general grant, b) grant for agriculture, c) disaster relief, d) grant aid for cultural activities, and e) food aid, etc.

-Technical Cooperation

Developing countries seek assistance for the improvement of social and industrial infrastructure. The field of technical cooperation covers from appropriate agricultural technologies, basic human needs of health and medical services to sophisticated computer science. There are various programs for developing countries such as trainee acceptance program, youth invitation program, expert dispatch program, equipment supply program, project-type technical cooperation, international emergency assistance, development studies, development cooperation program, and aid efficiency program.

-Direct Government Loans (ODA loans)

ODA loans are provided funds to developing countries at low interest rates and over long repayment periods.

-Aid through International Organizations

This type of aid is provided to the recipient countries through international organizations such as UN agencies like FAO, ILO, WHO, UNESCAP or ICA, ADB, APO, OECD, EL, ASEAN, etc.

Overview of International Aid

"…We pledge our political will and our common and national commitment to achieving food security for all and to an ongoing effort to eradicate hunger in all countries, with an immediate view to reducing the number of undernourished people to half their present level no later than 2015…."

According to DAC, the member-countries are requested to provide ODA equivalent to 0.5%(Criteria of UN : 0.7%) of their GNI. Nordic countries provide more than the criteria as shown in Table 17. The ODA provided by DAC (Development Assistance Committee of OECD) countries is fluctuating by economic condition. With a few exception, donors appear to be failing to live up to their commitments on aid volume even many commitments were reported such as **Rome Declaration on World Food Security**. Governments do not appear to be making the transition from rhetoric to action on poverty reduction, which is UN's overriding objective of MDGs. However, the Committee (DAC) of the OECD still appear to see economic adjustment and governance reforms as being the essentials of development. It is as if the alleviation of poverty is a bounce which is sure to follow. The rise in ODA from DAC donors of about one-half of 1% in real terms to a 2007 figure from $ 2,494 million; 0.94% of GDI(Norway) to$ 204million ; 0.07% of GDI(Poland), may mark the beginning of the new era of slowly growing ODA.

According to ODA volume and ODA as percentage of GDI in 2007 the largest country in ODA as percentage of GNI is Norway. However, USA and Japan are the largest donors in ODA volume in the year (Table17).

Table 17. ODA/GNI Ratio of OECD/DAC Countries (2007)

Rank	Nation	ODA(M$)	ODA/GDI(%)
1	Norway	2494	0.94
	Sweden	3397	0.94
3	Luxembourg	248	0.82
	Netherlands	5036	0.82
5	Denmark	2076	0.81
6	Belgium	1924	0.53

7	Austria	1539	0.52
8	France	9893	0.47
	England	10640	0.47
10	Finland	883	0.46
11	Switzerland	1757	0.44
12	Ireland	703	0.42
13	Germany	10013	0.36
14	Canada	3410	0.34
15	Italy	4958	0.29
16	Japan	13534	0.28
17	New Zealand	251	0.27
	Spain	2911	0.27
19	Australia	1577	0.25
20	United States	26888	0.22
21	Portugal	371	0.21
22	Iceland	27	0.18
23	Greece	372	0.17
	Turkey	601	0.17
25	Slovak Republic	56	0.12
26	Czech Republic	135	0.11
	Hungary	100	0.11
28	Korea	752	0.10
29	Poland	204	0.07
30	Mexico	No data	

Source: OECD, 2007.

History of Korea's ODA

As a recipient country, Korea received ODA from foreign countries total amount of 12 billion USD. Ranging from emergency relief to structural readjustment programs, ODA significantly contributed to Korea's economic and social development.

After the Korean War (1950~1953), ODA was the only source of capital, since the Korean economy had been almost devastated by the war. Much of the assistance in 1950s was focused on military support and humanitarian relief. Food aid and provision of daily necessities were also provided to meet the basic human needs. In the 1960s "growth" and "foreign investment" replaced "humanitarian relief" and "reconstruction" of war-torn country as Korea dramatically transformed its economic structure. Whereas ODA in the previous decade mostly took the form of grants to facilitate reconstruction, more concessional loans and other forms of financial investment came to Korea, allowing it to build social infrastructure and promote industrial development. In the 1970s and 1980s, stand-alone project financing introduced to heavy and chemical industries increasingly gave way to sector-wide loans or readjustment program loans aiming to reform the overall economic and industrial structure. The proportion of grants declined significantly and the sources of assistance continued to diversify. In the 1990s, Korea came to reverse its position from a recipient to a donor.

Korea ended its dependence on the World Bank's assistance in 1995 and was excluded from the DAC list of ODA recipients in 2000; however, Korea's history as a donor goes back to the 1960s.

In 1963 Korea hosted training program for public officials of developing countries for the first time funded by the U.S. To respond to the growing demand from partner countries, the Korean government gradually funded more of its assistance projects on its own budget. In 1977, as the first-ever assistance with official budget set aside for ODA, the Ministry of Foreign Affairs conducted equipment provision worth of 900 million KRW (about 2 million USD as of 1977). The amount of ODA provided by the Korean government reached a new peak in the late 1980s. Korea consolidated this significant shift by launching the Economic Development Cooperation Fund (EDCF) in 1987 and establishing the Korea International Cooperation Agency (KOICA) in 1991.

In 2010, Korea became the 24th member of the Development Assistance Committee (DAC), the international donor's club. Upon joining the OECD DAC in 2010, Korea has continuously improved its ODA system by enacting theFramework Act on International Development Cooperation (Framework Act), and devising the Strategic Plan for International Development Cooperation (Strategic Plan) as well as theMid-term ODA Policy for 2011-2015. Furthermore, Korea has worked to engage in the efforts of global development by leading the adoption of the Development Agenda at the G20 Seoul Summit in November 2010 and successfully hosting the Busan HLF-4 in November 2011, serving as a bridge among developed, emerging and developing countries, and leading the launching of Global partnership for Effective Development Cooperation.

International calls for sharing Korea's Experiences

"Korea, as the lighthouse for the developing countries, is required to share the experience of democratization and economic development" By Ban Ki-moon, UN Secretary-General (August 2011)

"Korea is able to pass on its experience in economic development and provides many lessons to developing countries" By Tony Blair, Former British Prime Minister (September 2011)

"I would like to implement Korea's Seamaul Undong in Africa because I believe it is a good example of how we can deal with poverty issue in such a poor country" by Jeffery Sachs, Columbua University(October 2011)

Legal framework

Korea enacted theFramework Act on International Development Cooperation (Framework Act) and the Presidential Decree which came into force in July 2010, and laid the legal basis for a more effective ODA system. The Framework Actdefines basic principles and objectives, role of the Committee for International Development Cooperation (CIDC), formulation of the Mid-term ODA Policy, roles and functions of agencies supervising international development cooperation, selection of priority partner countries, evaluation, support for civil organization, and public relations to enhanced transparency and people's participation. The Presidential Decree stipulates the detailed mandates for the enforcement of the *Framework Act.*

The *Framework Act* (Article 3) identifies the following five basic principles of the Korea's international development cooperation: (i) reduce poverty in developing co
untries; (ii) improve the human rights of women and children, and achieve gender equality; (iii) realize sustainable development and humanitarianism; (iv) promote cooperative economic relations with developing partners; and (v) pursue peace and prosperity in the international community. Under these principles, objectives of the Korea's International Development Cooperation are to achieve the following matters: (i) alleviate poverty and improve the quality of life of people in developing countries; (ii) support partner country's development and improve the system and conditions for such development; (iii) reinforce friendly relations with developing countries; (iv) contribute toward the resolution of global problems related to international development cooperation; and (v) other matters deemed necessary for realizing the basic principles. These visions are reflected in ODA policies and strategies and also repeatedly commented in various global fora on international development cooperation.

The Korean President's remarks at international conferences

Recognizing that narrowing the development gap is closely linked to the framework for strong, sustainable and balanced growth of the global economy, the Korean President suggested the promotion of a sustainable, inclusive and resilient growth in developing countries, and LDCs in particular as the goal of the Seoul Consensus on Development. < Letter of the President as the Chairperson of the G20 Seoul Summit (November 3, 2010) >

The Korean President shared some views on how to shape the future of international development cooperation as follows: (i) ownership of partner countries; (ii) inclusive development partnership; (iii) results-oriented development cooperation; (iv) accountable development cooperation; and (v) enhanced synergy among global fora < Keynote Speech in the Busan HLF-4 (November 30, 2011) >

In addition to the Framework Act and the Presidential Decree, there are several laws related to specific ODA agencies and activities. To introduce major regulations;

Act on the Measures for the Admission to International Financial Institutions (enacted in 1963) regulates the membership with the international financial institutions and measures to discharge the responsibilities as a member prescribed in the agreements governing the respective international financial institutions

Economic Development Cooperation Fund Act (enacted in 1987) regulates the establishment, operation and management of the Economic Development Cooperation Fund as concessional loan

Korea International Cooperation Agency Act (enacted in 1991) sets out the foundation of Korea International Cooperation Agency (KOICA) and its mandates to carry out grant aid projects and technical cooperation

Overseas Emergency Relief Act (enacted in 2007) prescribes the matters necessary for overseas emergency relief, such as dispatch of emergency relief teams, provision of emergency relief supplies, support for interim recovery from disasters, etc.

Sector

In 2008 and 2010, about 85% of total bilateral ODA was targeted to social and economic infrastructures development, with a sectoral focus on education, health, and transportation identified as priorities in partner countries' development strategies (Table18).

Table18 Bilateral ODA by Sector(2007-2011)(net disbursements, USD million, %)

	2007	2008	2009	2010	2011
Total	490.5 (100)	539.2 (100)	581.1 (100)	900.6 (100)	989.6 (100)
Social Infrastructure & Services	265.6 (54.1)	238.5 (44.2)	278.5 (47.9)	395.9 (44.0)	416.3 (42.1)
Education	105.1 (21.4)	62.3 (11.5)	71.9 (12.4)	146.3 (16.2)	179.4 (18.1)

Health	47.6 (9.7)	51.3 (9.5)	92.3 (15.9)	132.6 (14.7)	91.2 (9.2)
Population & Reproductive health	2.2 (4.3)	9.4 (1.7)	3.6 (0.6)	4.8 (0.5)	4.2 (0.4)
Water supply & Sanitation	21.3 (4.3)	43.2 (8.0)	41.5 (7.1)	53.7 (6.0)	71.7 (7.2)
Government & Civil society	86.0 (17.5)	62.7 (11.6)	61.5 (10.6)	49.0 (5.4)	53.1 (5.4)
Others	3.5 (0.7)	9.5 (1.8)	7.7 (1.3)	9.5 (1.1)	16.7 (1.7)
Economic Infrastructure & Services	104.2 (21.2)	124.1 (23.0)	152.7 (26.3)	250.2 (27.8)	308.2 (31.1)
Transport & Storage	41.4 (8.4)	75.6 (14.0)	77.4 (13.3)	117.7 (13.1)	229.8 (23.2)
Communications	34.7 (7.1)	46.1 (8.5)	59.6 (10.3)	63.4 (7.0)	40.0 (3.5)
Energy	25.1 (5.1)	-1.1 (-0.2)	14.2 (2.4)	64.6 (7.2)	35.0 (3.5)
Banking & Financing Services	1.9 (0.4)	2.6 (0.5)	0.9 (0.2)	2.0 (0.2)	1.5 (0.2)
Business & Other Services	1.0 (0.2)	0.9 (0.2)	0.5 (0.1)	2.4 (0.3)	1.9 (0.2)
Production Sectors	47.6 (9.7)	80.4 (14.9)	61.2 (10.5)	64.6 (7.2)	77.2 (7.8)
Agriculture, Forestry, Fishing	30.0 (6.1)	51.4 (9.5)	39.9 (6.9)	49.6 (5.5)	55.8 (5.6)
Industry, Mining, Construction	11.9 (2.4)	10.2 (1.9)	12.5 (2.1)	12.7 (1.4)	13.7 (1.4)
Trade Policies & Regulations	4.5 (0.9)	17.7 (3.3)	8.5 (1.5)	2.0 (0.2)	7.4 (0.7)
Tourism	1.2 (0.2)	1.2 (0.2)	0.4 (0.1)	0.3 (0.0)	0.4 (0.0)
Environment	5.2 (1.1)	7.2 (1.3)	8.7 (1.5)	14.4 (1.6)	16.9 (1.7)

Multi-sector/ Cross-cutting	11.4 (2.3)	17.4 (3.2)	29.2 (5.0)	104.6 (11.6)	56.0 (5.7)
Commodity aid/General Prog. Ass.	0.3 (0.1)	1.5 (0.3)	0.1 (0.0)	– –	1.9 (0.2)
Acting relating to debt	– –	10.3 (1.9)	0.0 (0.0)	2.7 (0.3)	– –
Humanitarian aid	17.1 (3.5)	24.0 (4.5)	17.0 (2.9)	17.9 (2.0)	24.1 (2.4)
Administrative costs	31.4 (6.4)	31.5 (5.8)	27.8 (4.8)	38.4 (4.3)	53.6 (5.4)
Unallocated & Unspecified	7.7 (1.6)	4.2 (0.8)	5.9 (1.0)	12.3 (1.4)	35.3 (3.6)

* Source: OECD, International Development Statistics Online DB

Bilateral ODA By sector (2007-2011) (Net Disbursements, USD million)

Korea has made progress in improving sector focus in its development cooperation. According to the *Mid-term ODA Policy for 2011-2015*, Korea continuously devotes grant aid to sectors such as education, health, governance, agriculture and fisheries, and industry and energy, in order to help partner countries achieve the MDGs and enhance their own growth potential. As for concessional loans, Korea plans to focus on building basic infrastructure which is indispensable for economic growth. To meet the recommendations of the DAC Special Peer Review in 2008, Korea also streamlined the sectoral focuses. The current CPS identifies only two to three priority sectors for each partner country in terms of division of labor and greater aid effectiveness.

Overview of Korean ODA

Korea has affirmed its commitment to increase its ODA volume. The commitment was echoed by the President at major international conferences including the UN General Assembly, the G20 Seoul Summit, Busan HLF-4. TheStrategic Plan also projects a steady increase of the ODA/GNI ratio up to 0.25% by 2015, by which Korea can come close to the average level of DAC members. Of note, Korea's ODA volume has increased in five consecutive years from USD 455 million in 2006 to USD 1,321 million in 2011, accomplishing the Korean government's commitment to the international community in the midst of the global economic crisis.

The Strategic Plan is stated to maintain the bilateral to multilateral ODA ratio at 70:30 in parallel with the steady increase in the total ODA volume by 2015.

Within bilateral ODA, Grants accounted for approximately 60-70% of Korea's bilateral ODA with slight variations in the past five years (2007-2011).

There is a trend in ODA volume vs. total fund rendered for developing countries, though the total fund has been increased on the contrary the ratio of ODA volume has been sharply decreased 1in some period, so far.

Korea has a remarkable and successful economic growth during the last four decades. As a result, many developing countries request Korea's economic and technical cooperation. However, the history of Korea's international cooperation is quite long.
Since Backje Dynasty Korea had transferred technologies to Japan without any royalty. And recently, Korea started international training programs at its own expenses in 1965. Programs for overseas dispatch of experts started in 1967. In 1977, with a budget of 900 million Won, Korea started to provide Korean machinery and materials to the developing countries in various fields.
In 1982, Korea launched an annual International Development Program to provide high ranking officials from the developing countries with invitational training based on Korea's development experience. Invitational trainings in various technologies for developing countries were also provided in 1983. The following year, provision of vocational training assistance was also started.
In order to meet these needs effectively, Korea established the Economic Development Cooperation Fund (EDCF) in 1987. The EDCF enabled Korea's provision of financial assistance and technological transfer more effectively.
In 1989, Korea started a communication technical assistance program, and in 1990, a program of overseas dispatch was carried out by dispatching Korea Young Volunteers for the first time to Southeast Asia.
Almost half of Korean ODA is rendered to the neighbor countries in Asia and Oceania. This trend is more or less similar with that of Japan.
Besides ODA, Korea has developed overseas' agriculture through direct investment. However, unstable political condition in some developing countries have hindered foreign investment.

Thanks mostly to the Semaul Undong, Korea has been remarkably developed in politics, economy and culture during the past 40 years and the country now takes the leading role among developing countries with the idea of **"From Recipient to Donor".** It has also brought tremendous changes to the most aspects of rural life and has had a considerable impact on social thoughts even outside of the country. From these reasons, Saemaul Undong has been spot lighted among the countries and they have sent community leaders and government officials to Korea and the numbers have been increased. Especially the political and rural community leaders of Asia, Africa, Central and South America who require to develop the national economy began to realize the importance of Saemaul Undong for the modernization of the rural communities and national development from aspect of the "on-the-spot experiences and training".

Saemaul Undong has become more pervasive into the world as a new model of a rapid national development so it is generally requested that Korea should keep close and positive relationship with those countries for the economic enrichment and diplomatic benefits in the international society. In order to know how to correspond with and what ways of methods for the international relationship, it is needed to research the structural and substantial ways to approach for their requirements as well.

General Concepts of International Cooperation of Saemaul Undong

For the International cooperation of Saemaul Undong, Public Relations activities of government level and international training of Saemaul Undong. It's one of the divisions "Department of International Cooperation" takes the key roles of planning, budgeting, education and programming regarding the international co-operative matters.

The Guidelines of International Cooperation

1) Escalation of International Exchange
2) Escalation of International Training Programme of Saemaul Undong
3) Escalation of Training programme of Saemaul Undong for the Overseas KoreansInternational Training Program of Saemaul Undong
4) Escalation of Relationship with existing foreign national movements
5) Introduction of Academic Seminars of Saemaul Undong
6) Effective control and organization of overseas Public Relations Team of Saemaul Undong

Since the establishment of KOICAinviting trainings are mostly carried out through KOICA. However ministries, local government, government corporations, universities and NGOs also are running their own programs for Saemaul eduction.

4. Discussion

As well known, combined aid from the world's NGOs in 1991 record US$ 5.2 billion made NGOs the fifth largest donors - above all except the USA, Japan, France and Germany. Given that at best perhaps 20% of official aid is targeted on poorer groups, NGOs may provide up to half of the aid to the poorest.

There are trends of increasing roles of NGOs in emergency assistance, linking long-term development processes and relationships between multilateral and bilateral aid agencies, and peace keeping forces.

Accordingly, ODA was required to establish close and effective relationships with NGOs in the aspects of the followings:

-The usefulness of governments and NGOs jointly supporting collaborative fund raising and a rationalization of labor encouragement specialization.
- The need to use, inter alia, monitoring and evaluation to enable NGOs and governments of appropriate tools for measuring social impact.
-The need to present definitions and methods of statistical reporting on NGOs employed by DAC members in order to increase transparency and comparability.

To support the collaborations sought between GOs and NGOs, there must be awareness on the following elements in the relationship:

-The mutual needs and benefits;
-The benefits of a pluralistic approach development by governments and NGOs;
-The need for inclusiveness, openness, honesty and transparency in their relationship and;
-The autonomy and independence of NGOs

Considering NGOs activities and ODA of Korea in terms of the volume, it is hardly compared with economically highly developed countries. Nonetheless, there is possibilities in Korean international cooperation for improvement of the efficiency, so far the authors have observed. However, it would be desirable to follow the model of Nordic countries in ODA in terms of programs and volume of finance.Accordingly, it is recommended that Korea should select programs such as poverty alleviation through Saemaul Undong including women in development and environmental education.

For the effective Korean ODA in the future, it is also recommended to strengthen NGOs and foster more volunteers for international cooperation through OJT for corporations and college education and so on.

In short, future direction of ODA could be summarized as follows;
○ Expansion of ODA
○ Establishment, of a System for Systemic Emergency Disaster Relief Activities
○ Improvement in Management
○ Increase in Public Awareness and Participation

As of 2009, there are many programs for foreigners i.e. one week program for the trainees from the Philippines, Tanzania, and Uganda was provided by Korean Saemaul Undong Center from March 22 to March 2

Those programs had started with disciplinary delegates from abroad as a chain of economic cooperation between Korea and foreign counties. The purpose of the program is to educate and convince the leaders of rural community development of the related countries and promote the international cooperation through the spirit of Saemaul Undong: diligence, self-help and cooperation. Hundreds of disciplines from dozens of countries have joined in the program and finished the course with success every year.

This training program had consequently brought about the senses on the necessity of Seamaul Undong for the developing countries through physical experience from success cases of actual community development leaders and showed them the fundamental character of Saemaul Undong thorough training and education. It also devoted for the participants to understand deeply about Korean's way of thinking and culture in broad aspect.

Considering globalization and multi-culture both of domestic and abroad, Saemaul Undong should find its new role expectation.

The Korean model of Saemaul Undong is in a transitional stage should take the shape of effective institutionalization, socialization and internalization, with desirable norms, structures and behavior cultivated by the movement in the globalized multi-culture society.

VII. Abstract and Emphases on Saemaul Undong

1. Abstract

New Community Movement of Korea(From Wikipedia)

The **New Community Movement** or **Saemaul Movement**, was a political initiative launched on April 22, 1970 by <u>South Korean presidentPark Chung Hee</u> (박정희, 朴正熙) to modernize the rural <u>South Korean economy</u>. The idea was based on the Korean traditional communalism called Hyang-yak (향약) and Doorae (두레), which provided the rules for self-governing and cooperation in traditional Korean communities. The movement initially sought to rectify the growing disparity of the <u>standard of living</u> between the nation's urban centres, which were rapidly industrializing, and the small villages, which continued to be mired in poverty. Diligence, self-help and collaboration were the slogans to encourage community members to participate in the development process. The early stage of the movement focused on improving the basic living conditions and environments whereas later projects concentrated on building rural <u>infrastructure</u> and increasing community income.[1] Though hailed as a great success in the 1970s, the movement lost momentum during the 1980s as economic situation and political environment in South Korea changed rapidly.

Overview

The movement promoted <u>self-help</u> and collaboration among the people, as the central government provided a fixed amount of raw materials to each of the participating villages free of charge and entrusted the locals to build whatever they wished with them. The government first selected 33,267 villages and provided 335 sacks of cement. 16,600 villages that demonstrated success were then granted additional resources of 500 sacks of cement and a ton of iron bars.

The New Community Movement did much to improve infrastructure in rural South Korea, bringing modernized facilities such as irrigation systems, bridges and roads in rural communities. The program also marked the widespread appearance of orange tiled houses throughout the countryside, replacing the traditional thatched or choga-jip houses. Encouraged by the success in the rural areas, the movement spread through factories and urban areas as well, and became a nation-wide modernization movement. However, the movement proved ultimately inadequate in addressing the larger problem of <u>migration</u> from the villages to cities by the country's younger demographic. Moreover, relatively low income in the rural area compared to the urban area became a major political issue in the late 1980s, one that no government intervention had been able to fully solve.[3] Although the Saemaul Movement has achieved a great success in reducing poverty and improving living conditions in rural areas, rapid industralization of South Korea changed the environment and diminished the momentum of the movement. The government-led movement with highly centralized organizations proved to be efficient in 1970s and early 80s, but it became less effective after Korea entered into more developed and industrialized stage. Also, the government-led centralized system brought corruption problems such as misuse of funding. Recognizing these problems, the Korean government changed the centralized structure of the movement by empowering civil society to lead the movement. Since 1998, the Saemaul Movement has entered into the second phase, focusing on new issues such as enhancing voluntary services in the community and international cooperation with developing countries.

The basic steps of the Saemaul Movement

Step 1: Basic Arrangements

1. Three arrangements for the start: People, Seed Money, Basic Principles
2. Forming a Core Group 1: Leaders
3. Forming a Core Group 2: Working Groups
4. Forming a Core Group 3: Applying the principles to existing organizations
5. Forming a Core Group 4: Sectional organizations
6. Raising Seed Money 1: Through sample cooperative projects
7. Raising Seed Money 2: By cooperative works

Step 2: Operation of the Project

1. Principles and standards for selecting projects
2. Planning a project
3. Persuading villagers 1 - Setting a model to villagers
4. Persuading villagers 2 - Encouraging 'you can do it' spirit
5. Collecting consensus 1- Small group meetings
6. Collecting consensus 2- General meeting of villagers
7. Let everybody play a their part
8. Preparing and managing the public property
9. Establishing the local Saemaul Movement center
10.Encouraging 'we are the one' spirit
11.Cooperating with other communities and the government

Step 3: Main Stage of the Project

1. Project 1 for living environment improvement: Improving the houses
2. Project 2 for living environment improvement: Eliminating inconveniences in the village
3. Project 3 for living environment improvement: Creating an environment for increasing income
4. Project 1 for income increase: Removing the obstacles
5. Project 2 for income increase: Launching cooperative projects
6. Project 3 for income increase: Commercializing things around you
7. Project 4 for income increase: Introducing new ideas
8. Project 5 for income increase: Modifying distribution system
9. Project 6 for income increase: Operating a factory
10. Consolidating community 1: Enhancing morals and communalism
11. Consolidating community 2: Providing a cultural center and other facilities
12. Consolidating community 3: Establishing a credit union

Step 4: Final Stage of the Project

1. Sharing the results and celebrating the success
2. Sharing the long-term prospects
3. Stabilizing of joint funds
4. Encouraging the Activities of sectional organizations
5. Regularizing meetings for technology research
6. Establishing a village hall
7. Publishing a local newspaper
8. Establishing a partnership with other regions and government offices
9. Setting up a sisterhood relationship with foreign countries

Going international

The Saemaul Movement has been accepted by the United Nations as one of the efficient rural development models in the world. The Economic Commission for Africa (ECA) has decided to select the Saemaul Movement as a base model for the Sustainable Modernization of Agriculture and Rural Transformation (SMART) program in 2008 Also, the movement has been exported to more than 70 countries, sharing the rural development experience world-wide.

2.Emphases on Saemaul Undong

As Pyeong Ik Choe discussed at the 2009 International Conference of Saemaul

Undong, writing ten papers is not so hard, but making a village better is very hard. So, we should learn from martial art masters. They never teach many skills for a beginner in a short time. Beginners should exercise step by step; start small, start slowly, otherwise the beginners would be confused. Through some 40 years of study and experience in rural Samaul Uundong, it was found that almost all successful villages developed agricultural technologies first and then set up marketing channels, so far. Recently he translated the ex-President Park's hand writing on Saemaul Undong. We can find his philosophy, the core concept and strategy and his emphasis on practice of Saemaul Undong(see the photo).

What is good life (wellbeing)?

○ Free from poverty...

○ Rual villages become rich, more relaxed and refined, and cultural life by income boosting

○ Love each other and mutual aid among villagers

○ Affordable and beautiful and livable village

Living well now is Important···but making better life for tomorrow, for our beloved descendants is more meaningful.(Let's find philosophical concept on Saemaul Undong.)

How to live well?

(1) All know how, problem is practice.

(2) Diligence makes rich

(3) Strong spirit of self reliance makes rich

(4) Strong cooperative spirit of all villagers makes rich

One family member is not workable

All family members should be diligent

One family is not enough

All villagers should be diligent

When all villagers are diligent they are more cooperative in practice of Saemaul Undong(see the photo).

Again Pyeong Ik Choe emphasized practical rather than theoretical at the
Global Saemaul Forum(27~29, Gyeongju, Korea) such as; Now we have

more than enough knowledge, history, sprit and strategy on Saemaul Undong. What to do from now on? We need to learn from martial art masters.

There are only 3 tips in boxing— straight, upper cut, hook and the difference between champion and looser is practice. Successful Saemaul leaders also practice for their dreams and never give up it.

In short, this way of sharing development experience would be available for the many who are poor in the huts and villages in the world. However if we want the same result as Korean Saemaul Undong in abroad, we need to make the same condition as 1970s' Korea. The drawing shows the concept.

Recently Korea dispatchesmany experts such as World Friends and ODA specialists for the developing countries in various fields. Dr. Pyeong Ik Choe also has been to the Ministry of Local Government of Rwanda as a volunteer. And Dr. Chan-Ho Choi has dedicated to ICA as the Chancellor of Asian ICA in New Deli , Dr. Chi-Sun Oh the founder of KICU, Dr. Badar N. Siddiqui has long experience in extension service of Pakistan and Dr. Jaydip Mehta has studied and taught in both of Korea and India. From their experiences in Asia and Africa, some idea would be availablefor the new volunteers.

In addition, wishes to see many more young Korean volunteers serving to Africa a, Asia and Latin America with sweat, tears and prayer areincluded too.

From this point of view several development strategies for developing countries were attached as appendix.

REFERENCES

가나안농군학교, 1990,가나안복민운동 1,2

김영환,1959, 덴마크 갱생운동사, 신교출판사

매헌기념사업회, 1986,매헌유고

백승구(편), 1985,심훈의재발견, 미문출판사

심훈(인주승편), 1992, 상록수외 최용신의생애 홍익재

안창호, 1974,도산안창호 논설집, 을유문화사,

오치선, 1977, "도시학교 새마을교육의 새로운 방향 설정에 관한 연구", 연세교육과학 제
　　11집, 연세대학교 교육대학원

외솔회, 2002, 나라사랑 제104집

최병익, 2010, 새마을운동-평가와전망,도서출판 세왕최병익, 2014, "새마을운동의 세계화
　　와 심훈 상록수 교육", 한국의 인간 상록수 전기 (사)심훈 상록수 기념사업회

통계청, 2007, 지방자치단체 외국인 주민현황

Ahmad, Rai Niaz and Choe, P. I., 2014, "Sharing Development Experience of
　　PakistanUniversity's Outreach and Saemaul Undong", Presented at Global
　　Saemaul Forum, Aug27~29, Gyeongju, Korea..

Aqua, Ronald, "Role of Government in the Saemaul Movement," edited by Lee, Man
　　Gap 1981,Toward a New community Life.

Cheong, J. W.,1987, Promising Education for Community Development, Seoul National
　　University Press.
　　Korean Overseas Information Service, 1995. Facts about Korea

Guyer, D. L. and Frarey, M. E., "Function of Private Voluntary organizations within the
　　Saemaul Movement", edited by Lee, M. G., 1981, Toward a New Community
　　Life.

Jacob, P. E., et al, Values and the Active Community, the Free Press, 1971

Jeon, D. I., et. al., The Role of Saemaul Credit Unions In Regional Community
　　Development, Saemaul Undong English Summaries of Reseach Articles on
　　Saemaul Undong, Volume 12, The Headquarters of Saemaul Undong, 1986.

Kee, Youngwha, Saemaul Education; Past & Present, 2009 International Conferance of
　　Saemaul Undong.

Kim, S. S. and Cheong, J. W., "Saemaul Training as an Educational Innovation,"
　　Innovative Community Development, edited by Lee, J. H. 1983, Institute of
　　Saemaul Undong Studies, Seoul National University.

Lee, J. H. and Rozen P., "Prospects of the Saemaul Undong,"edited by Lee, Man-Gap
　　1981, Toward a New Community Life.

Lee, J. H., "Review of Saemaul Undong: Impacts and Its Implications," Iedited by Lee, J.
　　H. 1983, Innovative Community Development,.

Oh, Chi-Sun, 1977, "A Taxonomical Study Concerning the Establishment of a
　　New Direction for Saemaul Education in the Urban Schools of
　　Korea" Yonsei Science of Education, Vol.11, Yonsei University

Park, J. H., 1979,"Introduction," Seamaul: Korea's New Community.

Park, J. H., "Saemaul Undong and Korean National Development," Choe, Y. B.,
　　1978,The Korean Model of Rural Saemaul Undong, Working Paper 4, Korean
　　Rural Economics Institute. Edited by Lee, J. H., 1983, Innovative Community
　　Development.

Reed, Edward P, "Village Cooperation and the Saemaul Movement," edited by Lee, M. G., 1981, Toward a New Community Life.

Toynbee, A. J., A Study of history, Abridgement of Vol. I -VI, Oxford Univ. Press, 1947.

www.cu.co.kr

www.kor-canaan.or.kr

www.koica.go.kr

www.kostat.go.kr

www.mosa.go.kr

www.nonghyup.com

APPENDIX : How to Accelerate Development of Rwanda

Preface

This booklet suggests some alternatives as countermeasures to challenges of Rwanda.

As I say often the lord gives not only challenges but also alternatives. Hence what we have to do is finding the optimal alternatives solving the challenges. From this point of view Rwanda blessed all alternatives.

Sometimes outsiders can see clearly the forest than insiders.

I suggested 1 to 1 system to develop Rwanda. However those ideas are not my own unique ones. Among others, I got the idea of "1 to 1" from "1 cow 1 family". The other ideas also were found among alternatives already blessed in Rwanda..

I have done my best and have walked almost every day around 8 kilometers so that I could meet so various Rwandan and became familiar with Rwandan culture to cook agatogo by myself..

Before this booklet I suggested around 10 strategies to accelerate Rwandan development. The suggestions were printed in 500 calendars and distributed to almost of all government organizations from central to local.

In this booklet 9alternatives in 3 fields were emphasized.

To empower human capital thru establishment of Rwanda Development Institute, week-end graduate schools and credit accumulation systems (*Improving accessibility to higher education opportunity)*

To develop new bread baskets. thru more rice in marsh land, developing silk and orchid industry*(Developing high value commodities*.)

To boost tourism thru contents development, theme parks (orchid park & international cultural park),handicraft design clinic and enhancing logos (*Attracting tourists*.). Recently I traveled Uganda and Kenya to see flower industry without any support. However it's more convinced that exporting Rwandan orchids is so much promising though they are sleeping up to now.

I often say, " farmers are better than professors and government officers, since there is no guarantee of next income for farmers so they use brain and try more compared with the *iron balls* " and ' me also a professor, an iron ball.'

During field tour I had car accident of upside down but nobody wounded. I believe the lord allowed more chance to dedicate for the developing countries as the 16 countries did for Korea during and after Korean War. I never forget it. Now my turn to return the love.

June 25 at Ministry of Local Government, Rwanda

With thanks to the both of Rwanda and KOICA Professor Pyeong Ik CHOE, Ph.D.

TABLE OF CONTENT

I. HOW TO EMPOWER HUMAN CAPITAL?

1.ESTABLISHMENT OF RWANDA DEVELOPMENT INSTITUTE (RDI)

As emphasized in the report of Rwandan Vision 2020, low human capital is one of the most challenging constraints in national development. To solve this problem, some development models were bench marked such as Singapore and Korea. Among others, Korea has very much similar with Rwanda in terms of history and national development strategies. Especially, Umuganda is so similar with Korean Saemaul Undong.

Besides Saemaul Undong, Korea established Korea Development Institute(KDI) 1n 1971 (the same year of the launch of Saemaul Undong) to study national development policy and to provide degree course to meet the needs of higher education. As Korea accomplished in national development, it's desirable to establish RDI to accelerate Rwandan development through policy study and empowering government staffs.

OBJECTIVES

The objectives to establish RDI is accelerating Rwandan development and in particular the RDI has the following aims:

i. To provide research and analysis of development policy for government, private corporations, and the general public.

ii. To provide a program of study for community development to meet the needs of empowerment of government staffs and community leaders for national development through professional training for vision 2020 and onwards.

DEGREE PROGRAM STRUCTURE

The program consists of eight modules with 3 credits each and dissertation has no credit (only Pass or Fail). Each module is taught equivalent period to fifteen weeks and three hours each week. The minimum credits for the degree require 24credits (8 credits during each of semester 1~ 3) except thesis. The individual dissertation write up period can be conducted in semester 2 according to the approval of advisor professor. This translates to minimum program for excellent student requires three semesters (twelve months).

The following modules shall be offered for MA degree:

ICT, Community development policy and strategy, Social Protection Policy and implementation plan, Regional Planning and Infrastructure, Globalization and Industrial Policy, Agribusiness and Processing, Environment and Energy Policy, Community Education and Dissertation.

The total modules and credits are the same systems of Korea, Japan, USA and other global systems : 8 modules (24 credits → MA degree (equivalent to 180 credits of current Rwandan system

+ 12 modules(36 credits→Ph. D. degree).

The following table shows modules of required courses and some electives should be offered to meet the needs of students.

Table Modules, Credits per Semester for MA Degree

	modules	credits	Faculty
1st semester	Communitydevelopment policy and strategy,	3	
	Social Protection and implementation plan	3	
	Community Education,		
		3	
2nd semester	Regional Planning and Infrastructure, Globalization and Industrial Policy, Agribusiness and Processing	3	
		3	
		3	

3rd semester	ICT	3	
	Environment and Energy Policy	3	
	Seminar		
	Dissertation	1	
		0	
total		24	

When MA degree holders continue to study and get 12 modules with dissertation of doctoral thesis will probably be given Ph. D. Degree by the RDI Committee.

Modules for MA and Ph. D. degrees should be developed/modified and submitted to the RDI Committee before 1 month to the beginning of new courses.

ADMISSION REQUIREMENT

Candidates to MA will be selected on the basis of their performance in the undergraduate degree (BSc or BA) in the following fields plus at least 2 years experience as a government officer..

i.community development, development studies, agribusiness, education, engineering and industrial policy development administration, et.c.

ii.Students including foreigners with BA are acceptable if they have at least 2 years experience in the field of international cooperation.

Ph. D. course will be offered just after the first MA course finished.

LOCATION AND TEACHING DAYS

i. Location : MINALOC

ii. Teaching Days and Hours

Friday: Afternoon (Sportsl Activity Time)

Saturday: Full Day (9:00 a.m. to 6:00 p.m.)

FACULTY

Full time professor : World Friends Korea of KOICA

Part time professor : professor of KIST, NUR, I.S.A.E., KIE, et.c.

Teaching assistant : internship

SELECTION METHOD

Graduate School Authority will select among applicants recommended by Ministers. And the following number of enrollment also will be decided by the Authority.

MA : Around 20, foreigners are additionally acceptable

Ph.D: Around 10,   ---- Do ---

ROAD MAP :

Decree → Cabinet → Parliament → HE President → Course Establishment → Selection of Applicants → Course Beginning

EXPECTED RESULTS

- Empowerment of government staffs is expected
- For excellent staffs, no need to leave their work to study abroad, at least 2(MA)~ 5(MA+Ph.D) years
- Synergy effect in the development of a national network is expected
- Enhancing Rwandan government staffs to top level in Africa is prospected

2. IMPROVING ACCESSIBILITY TO HIGHER EDUCATION AND CREATIVE EDUCATION

One of the most important factors concerning national development as well as individual family's wellbeing is education. In this point of view improving accessibility to higher education is so desirable approach.

Through education Rwanda can catch up developed countries from one of "seventeen emergingcountries of Africa."

1).WEEK-END GRADUATE SCHOOL OF EDUCATION IN KIE

Our future depends on the growing children. Accordingly the education in KIE is so important. Further more on the job training and degree course for teachers are also desirable. For teachers, week end degree courses is needed in the aspect of the fast developing world in terms of new knowledge.

2). STRENGTHENING KIGALI CAMPUS OF ISAE

The population of Rwanda would be doubled by 2030. That means Rwanda needs to produce two hundred percent of food compared with the volume of currently producing food. Otherwise Rwanda should import the huge volume of food from global food market.

To strengthen food security, higher agricultural education and extension education also should be strengthened

From this point of view it would be available to reform the Kigali campus of I.S.A.E. into collage of agricultural education and extension as well as week end graduate school.

Doing so Rwanda can more easily accomplish self sufficiency of food. Furthermore exporting orchid and high value processed food produced by MSes also would be realized in the near future.

Among others art and design education also will be included in the modules since technologies enhance added value of commodity and arts maximize the added value.

3). ADOPTION OF MODULE-CREDIT ACCUMULATION SYSTEM

Many Rwandan schools offer evening classes for working students. It's very much desirable. However compared with ten million population, the number of universities and colleges is not enough for the need of higher education in the aspect of fast developing Rwanda.

If module-credit system is available, poor or working students can continue their studies in higher education institute such as community colleges as well as universities, even in graduate schools.

For example, students cannot pay full tuition fee in some semester or some year but if they can afford one or two modules, they can study one or two subjects. Doing so, even the total periods of their enrollment are much longer than full time students, any way they can continue higher education.

Democratic welfare society is nothing but an accessible society in any aspect.

4). STRENGTHENING CREATIVE EDUCATION

For the question, 'what is development?", several sharp students from a top level university answered all the same such as " process!". That is the result of the limitation of modules they study. Without varieties of electives, in other words, with all the same modules, education is like a biscuits factory producing only one kind.

Broader thinking and creativeness should be grown by offering varieties of electives.

Thru education of poem, music and drawing beautiful soul and creativeness should be grown especially in primary and secondary education.

Doing so Rwandan Michael Jackson also could be grown and growing Rwandan Harry Potter could be also possible. As well known the author, Joanne K. Rowling earns as much as one of the biggest global companies.

If those schools in England and USA were mono type biscuit factories, could they had grown their world renowned artists?

II. HOW TO DEVELOP NEW BREAD BASKETS?

As often said, those expressions of 'god is food', 'eating first', ' think food as heaven' are common all over the world. Of course there is no ague food security is most essential among others especially in developing countries.

1. FROM MARSH LAND TO RICE FIELD

Morethanhalfoftheworld'spopulationdependsmostlyonriceasastaplefood. And rice consumption in Rwanda has been increasing. However new bread baskets for Rwandan were already blessed. Lowlandriceisgrownmostlyonratherheavyclay.Itcanbegrownthroughouttheyearprovidedthereisasuffici entsupplyofwaterora relativelyabundantrainfall-particularlyduringthegrowingstage. Hence paddy farming in marsh land of Rwanda is so ideal.

THE SUCCESS OF GIHOGWE

As reported in the home page of MINALOC(24 may, 2012), Gihogwe village showed the potential of marsh land as Rwandan's a new bread basket.

In Gihogwe village, five young volunteers(team leader : SHON Daeho) from Korea made participatory plans with 60 famers(now 100) among 250 families to develop marsh land to rice field in December, 2011 .

They set up rice cooperative (COODARIKA) and studied how to farm and cooperatively developed rice field as well as improved river to prevent flood. Doing so they made small but very much promising miracle merely by their own hand without any farm machine.

By around August they will harvest the first rice. When they develop 15ha of rice field, the rice cooperative members can make 200~300US$ as additional annual farm income.

INTEGRATED COMMUNITY DEVELOPMENT

Education to eradicate illiteracy and malnutrition and educationon sanitation and vegetable growing are also caring out in the village center. The center was constructed currently using 54,000US$ supported by Kyeongbuk Province, Korea.

The Korean young volunteers together with villagers are planning to establish rice-cooperative's office and rice-drying place. Improving irrigation and developing threshing machine are also included in their plan.

Let's go in field! Rehabilitation begin

2012/04/28 16:27

Mr. LEE Sangan of KOICA is advising volunteers in Gihogwe

> *One more bread basket eradicating absolute poverty and malnutrition is 1 cow 1 family program so far. For the more successful development of this program, building dairy cooperative would be available for newly involved area. Intensive extension education and policies upgrading the breed also should be continued.*

2. BUILDING RWANDAN SILK ROAD

According to LEE Sangan of KOICA and SOHN KeeWook of Korea Sericulture Association, Rwanda is one of the most ideal countries for sericulture

WHY SILK?

Silk has the following characteristics:

-Symbol of noble class an rich,

-Good for skin,

-Good for coloring,

-Byproducts and medical use

In the beginning, silk from silk worm will be produced and

in the long run high value silk products with Rwandan brand should be developed. Art will make it possible and transportation cost is nothing for high quality design.

WHY ART?

Technology enhance added value,

Art maximize added value.

BENCH MARKING

- Thomson Silk Co in Thai, and

- Hanse Co in USA : 5 cloths are sold per second in USA made by Hanse (Korean company)

WHY NOT RWANDA? RWANDAN CAN DO IT!

A silk project launched in Rwanda recently by MINAGRI with cooperation of Korea. It will realize Rwandan Silk Road in the near future.

Mr. LEE Sangan of KOICA and director SOHN Kee Wook of Korea Sericulture Association, searching for ideal land .

3. ESTABLISHMENT OF ORCHID EXPORTING SYSTEM

Considering Rwandan climate and comparing that of Thai, it's convinced the future of Rwandan orchid is so much promising. Accordingly a new project proposal for Rwanda next to the establishment of RWANDA DEVELOPMENT INSTITUTE (RDI), is ESTABLISHMENT of ORCHID EXPORTING SYSTEM (EOES).

From the above mentioned view of point, the multi-dimensional project is suggested: empowerment of staffs as well as cooperative leaders (MINALOC), boosting tourism and management of orchid park to be constructed(RDB), orchid education in secondary school(MINEDUC), extension education for farmers and management of the research center to be established(MINAGRI) and establishment of exporting system, et. c.

EXPECTED RESULT

Basically it's expected to boost rural income and orchid will enhance Rwandan economy thru especially exporting and tourism.

Location of Research Center and Orchid Park

The location for orchid-research center and orchid park is recommended around Volcanoes National Park in the aspect of good climate for orchid as well as synergy effect of tourism.

RECOMMENDATIONS

A task force team including the concerning ministries is needed for the preparation of Project Concept Note (project proposal) to be submitted to KOICA.

Besides orchid, mum, lily, rose and herbs should be included in the project..

WHAT IS ORCHID?

The orchid family is aflowering plant with colorful and fragrant bloomsbetween 21,950 and 26,049 species species, found in 880 genera. Bulbopyllum is the largest genera (2,000 species), Epidendrum (1,500 species), Dendrovium (1,400 species) and Pleurothallis (1,000 species)

The family includes vanilla(the genus of the vanilla plant), Orchis(type genus), Phalenopsis and Cattleya. Since the introduction of tropical species in the 19th century, horticulturists have produced more than 100,000 hybrids and cultivars.

- tropical Asia: 260 to 300 genera
- tropical America: 212 to 250 genera
- **tropical Africa: 230 to 270 genera**
- Oceania: 50 to 70 genera
- Europe and temperate Asia: 40 to 60 genera
- North America: 20 to 26 genera (From Wikipedia)

WHY ORCHID?

Beauty(flower of flower) and romantic aroma(not all)Very

long flowering periodSome orchids are used as medicine and food,

Live on the trees and stones→make fantastic,

High quality (elegant, luxurious)→expensive (25~75$/pot in USA, Europe, Korea & Japan, some orchids are sold at the price of 100$ and over),

Easy to grow and no need expensive tools,

Can be produced in a small area so even youths without any land can grow many orchid under trees, on the walls and under the roofs,

Small, light → *almost of all countries export by air plain, so landlocked countries can compete with seashore* countries.

BENCH MARKING

Thai orchid: shares 35% of world market and in case of phalenopsis occupies 80%. Around year 2000 Thai exported 100 million US$ of orchid..

Uganda produces vanilla orchid and Ugandan government recommends to produce more for enhancing farm income. In Uganda consumers buy vanilla seed to use it as tea

Only think of vanilla ice cream it's enough to imagine the huge volume of global vanilla market. Hence Rwanda should consider to develop local market as well as world market in terms of vanilla orchid.

Flowers mostly are exported by air all over the world. Kenya also exports flowers by air even she has ports. . As far as flower concerns, land locked country is meaningless. Accordingly Rwanda and Uganda can compete with seashore countries in global flower markets.

The flower industry of Kenya is the second largest agricultural foreign exchange earner after tea and revenues of 250 million US$ a year.

In Rwanda   some farmers are in Lurindo district and some NGO such as Imbabazi (orphanage)   in Rubavu district is growing flowers to sell. And the Imbabazi has two species of orchid. But orchid in Rwanda is not yet sold except in a flower shop in Kigali. Even Imbabazi has a wonderful orchid garden.

Vanilla dealer in Kampala

A flower company in Nairobi connects flowers to airplanes to export.

WHY NOT RWANDA?

Flower market in Rwanda now is in a initial stage comparatively, however the potential of Rwandan flower industry in particular exporting orchid is very much promising in the aspect of climate of Rwanda.

Researches were conducted by orchid pioneers such as **Merlo T. Nicole** (1942~2010). Among others she collected about 200 genera of orchid and has conserved those so valuable orchids in her   house in Gisenyi. She really dedicated to Rwandan orchid history. Now those orchids are caring by her son and her student..

DELEPIERRE Gilbert, LEBEL Jean Paul(2003) surveyed Rwandan orchids and reported 40 genera with 212 species.
Eberhard Fisher and Thorothee Killmann(2008) well illustrated orchids in their book, : Plants of Nyungwe National Park Rwanda .

Recently exporting roses to Europe was conducted by Beatrice Gakuba, however more varieties of flowers such as orchids, mums and lilies should be pursued.
Business only can hardly go far without strengthening the potential of grass root farmers as well as youth education.

Now it's time to set up exporting system of Rwandan orchid.
For this great launch the following preparation is needed:

- **Orchid education for farmer (on the job training),**
- **Orchid education for student and youth,**
- **Continuing and more systematic research by an orchid park (to be established including research center, training center, packing and exporting facilities and cultural garden, et. c.)**

III. ENHANCING TOURISM

The main trends of the world tourism are divided into twelve specific fields of tourism as follows:.
① ecotourism is one of the fastest growing areas
② safe Islamic countries will lead to an increase .
③over crowdedness in famous places
④ increase in tourism in under developed/closed areas
⑤development of dual forms of air travel : one form with a comfortable and high quality service and the low-cost air travel

⑥smaller, fasterSNSby the development of mobile phone and laptop makes a business trip like a vacation

⑦increase in high-quality hotel guests

⑧ increase in cruise travel

⑨ growing demand herb and massage at the spa for holidays

⑩increase in service andeducation tourism

⑪increase in silver-age tourist and women-only items

(Newsweek, July 22/29 2002)

According to the above trends of tourism, the future of Rwandan tourism is so much promising.

As reported in Hope Magazine(May 2011) by Fred Oluochi-Ojiwah, Rwanda's tourism industry brought into the economy over US$56million up during the first quarter of 2011 from US$43 million during the same period of 2010.

This increment in particular caused by new contents such as the canopy walkway in Nyungwe National Park, Akagera National Park and Volcanoes National Park and so on.

However there are much room to develop Rwandan tourism through contents development without huge investment.

Some alternatives boosting tourism could be recommended as the followings.

1. CONTENTS DEVELOPMENT

If the more contents could be developed it would be better for boosting tourism.

Among numerous cultural assets in Rwanda, the traditional wedding ceremony is so attractive for foreign tourists.

2. CONSTRUCTION OF THEME PARK

More theme parks such as cultural parks are recommendable. In the cultural parks, sculptures and rocks carved with environment friendly/ romantic poetry/ songs might be established. Among those works foreigners' poetry and songs also should be included for instance : poems of

Tagore(India), Li Po(China), Basho(Japan), Robert Frost (USA), Songs of the Beatles (UK) and Michael Jackson(USA) and so on.

However if the concepts of those poems and songs are harmonizing with the places it would be much better.For instance, the following poem will be available for around Mountain Gorilla Park..

COME TO MUSANZE
        Pyeong Ik CHOE

Come to Musanze city.
Come to Musanze in the Lord's forest.

You will be a princess of the forest and
A prince riding on a white horse in Musanze.

The ancient sun lights shine
Mountain Karisimbiand Lake Burera
Send fresh air to wash the fatigue..

A deep breath explains enough
Why the mountain gorillas live here

3. MORE LOGOS AND HANDCRAFT DESIGN CLINIC

Currently the mountain gorilla is representing Rwandan tourism in terms of logo. Though the gorilla logo is good, howeverthe following logos : **land of orchid** and **land of aroma** are recommended. Since there are many more attractive places and resources for the tourists in Rwanda.

land of orchid

The logo, **land of orchid** was designed by a Korean designer **Namyoung KIM** for Rwanda.

LET'S MAKE LAND OF AROMA

If more herb flowers such as orchid and night flower are planted in every corner of Rwanda it will make Rwandan tourism more fantastic. Especially night flower produces aroma after sunset to sunrise. Even cut flower also fills all room with aroma all night.

Without any huge invest it's possible to plant orchid and night flower in every corner in Rwanda within 2~3 years. It will boost tourism.

LET'S IMPROVE HANDICRAFT DESIGN

Some beautifully designed handicraft is made with **cow dung**. No matter how beautiful the design is tourists hardly could buy if they had known what the material is. The material should be changed.

Wood Gorilla, traditional **Agaseke** and **Drum** are very beautiful items in any aspect.

However quality improvement is needed in the aspect of design and strength in some handicrafts such as **ceramics**.

Saemaul Undong and Rural Development

Pyeong Ik Choe. Ph.D.
Professor & Director of Saemaul Education Center, KICU
PM, KOICA Project of Agriculture Univ. Rawalpindi, PK
Ex Dean, College of Pmas Arid Industrial Sci &Graduate School of Indstrial. Sci, KNU

Chi-Sun Oh, Ph.D.
Chancellor, Korea International Culture University of Graduate
Professor, Myong Ji University
Dean, Graduate School of Education &Graduate School of Social Education, Myong Ji Univ.
President, Korean Youth Research Association
President, World Association of Youth Sciences

Chan Ho Choi, Ph.D.
Vice President, Korea Institute for Rural Development
Ex Regional Director for Asia-Pacific, ICA
Ex Vice President of Academic Affairs, Agricultural Cooperative Univ, NACF

Badar N. Siddiqui, Ph.D
Associate Professor & Chairman of Dept of Agri Extension
Pmas Arid Agriculture University Rawalpindi, Pakistan